Essay Becomes Easy

Part II

Cause and Effect * Critical * Deductive * Definition
Descriptive * Expository * Informal

By EssayShark

Copyright Page

This book is protected by copyright law. You cannot use it for any purposes other than informational. Neither the entire book nor its parts can be resold, copied, reproduced or transmitted in any form or any means without permission of the rights holder. By reading this note you agree that the author is not responsible for your academic success. Usage of all the recommendations given in the book does not guarantee high academic scores.

Table of Contents

Introduction

Secondly, our book is suitable for all students — those in high school, college, and university. No, you didn't miss anything. That was really the first sentence. "Then why 'secondly?'" you wonder. This is because "firstly" refers to our first book and this is already the second one. Our two books are connected by the same topic (how to write essays), but they are different.

In our previous book, you can read guides on analysis, classification, persuasive, evaluation, compare and contrast, reflective, and narrative essays, while in this book, there are other types of essays, such as definition, critical, deductive, descriptive, expository, informal and cause and effect essays. It is very likely that you will need to complete essays of all types while studying. Therefore, we recommend to purchase both of our books.

In each book, you will find full tutorials on writing certain types of essays and high-quality samples on each type of essay. Therefore, you will be able to see how theoretical rules can be applied in practice. Also, we'll provide you with interesting topics on each type of essay so that you won't need to look for topics each time you write an essay.

And finally, we have prepared a kind of surprise for you. The surprise is hidden in the text that you've just read. Letters in bold make a sentence. Have you found it? We hope you already understand that we tried to wish you good luck! Be attentive while reading *Essay Becomes Easy. Part I* and *Essay Becomes Easy. Part II* and you will find a lot of interesting and useful information!

Chapter 1. Cause and Effect Essay Writing Guide

Among young people, there is a widespread opinion that writing a good essay about causes and effects is comparable with the name of a famous movie — *Mission: Impossible*. However, this is actually much easier than it might seem. Choose a good topic, think a little about the points and use your mind — that is the recipe of a well-prepared cause and effect essay. This guide was written to facilitate and speed up this process for you.

What's So Special About a Cause and Effect Essay?

A cause and effect essay represents just exactly what its title suggests — the main purpose of this paper is to explain what the reasons are for a special problem, and then state what the possible consequences are of this problem. Without a doubt, this explanation is quite understandable; however, to soothe my conscience, some additional thought about this type of paper should be stated. First of all, you should clearly understand what both "cause" and "effect" mean (considering them separately). A cause is usually conceived as a phenomenon, the outcome of which produces, determines or causes another phenomenon, and the result can be defined as an

4

effect. Joined together, the cause and effect process represents a fundamental law of nature and the basic logical category of connection. This law works regardless of your desire, while the understanding of this relationship only proves your ability to think, draw conclusions, and build logical chains.

Another point that should be addressed includes several types of effects and several types of causes that are better to be taken into consideration (Jennifer, 2014). These types are as follows:

Primary — the most significant and meaningful ones.

Contributory — can be called additional, and is the opposite category of primary.

Remote — describes less obvious causes or effects; also consists of some factors with which the relations are indirect (by means of other causes or effects).

Immediate — the ones that produce an effect in the short-term perspective.

The last additional point that will be addressed before moving on to structure and writing stages is the types of cause and effect essays. Even though we are accustomed to the fact that both cause and effect are in tandem, students can easily be confused by the terms. It is quite a common situation for students to be required to write an essay either about causes or effects of some phenomenon (this will be reflected in the proposed topics for your cause and effect essay in the Guidelines and Tightening Your Essay section of this guide). Regarding this, please note that a cause and effect essay reflects the type of relation (logic connection) between issues in the text. However, there can be several types of such link — for example, there might be several causes that contribute to a single effect and vice versa (Cause and Effect Essay, 2015).

Compare:

Causes — being good at languages; admiring world-known authors; taking part in several literature contests. Effect — the decision to enter a bachelor program in literature.

Cause — medical reform. Effects — lower prices for insurance and medicines; greater availability for various population groups; increase in the number of working hours for medical workers.

Cause and Effect Essay Writing Structure

The basic structure of cause and effect essays is just the same as the traditional structure of any essay writing types, with an attractive introduction, reasonable body, and clear conclusion. At the same time, depending on the topic and the mentioned types of papers (differentiated by the number of causes and effects), you may use three patterns of construction for your future cause and effect essay (How to Write a Cause and Effect Essay on Any Topic, n.d.).

1. Multiple causes & effect.

As you have already guessed, the variations in structure between several types of cause and effect essays are in the body — the theme of body paragraphs, to be more specific. In this particular type, each paragraph is devoted to one of the causes and can be supported with the minor ideas. Here, your attention should be paid to the explanation of both major and minor points, which should be written in an understandable manner.

In this case, *the thesis statement* is presented in this form: Phenomenon is caused by Cause 1, Cause 2, Cause 3.

Body paragraphs should be structured the following way:

I. Cause 1

    A. Minor idea 1.1

    B. Minor idea 1.2

II. Cause 2

    A. Minor idea 2.1

    B. Minor idea 2.2

III. Cause 3

    A. Minor idea 3.1

    B. Minor idea 3.2

2. Cause & multiple effects.

If the topic assumes that there are several effects of a single issue, the first step is to identify all of the issues (at least several of them). This structure also suggests group effects connected with each other in two or three main points, which will be supported by minor supports (the effects itself). Do not forget to give examples and explanations to each thought.

The general outline for this type of paper will be:

Thesis statement: Phenomenon has three groups of effects.

I. Group 1

    A. Effect 1.1

    B. Effect 1.2

II. Group 2

    A. Effect 2.1

    B. Effect 2.2

III. Group 3

    A. Effect 3.1

    B. Effect 3.2

3. Causal chain / domino.

This pattern presents a situation when each effect becomes a cause for the next one. This scheme is quite similar to a chain of dominoes (especially when you need to discuss the causes and effects of some negative issue — you may draw a parallel with the falling domino chain).

In this pattern, the events lead to one another, as in the following organization:

Cause 1 leads to Effect 1.

Effect 1 (Cause 2) leads to Effect 2.

Effect 2 (Cause 3) leads to Effect 3.

The thesis statement for this case in the general form can be represented as follows: Cause 1 leads to Effect 3.

The biggest challenge for this type of structure for a cause and effect essay is to sustain the logic while proving the main idea. At the same time, this pattern is the most creative and gives an opportunity to prove even the most "insane" theories and connections. The main requirement here is credible testimony in the form of examples, statistics, and research.

Stages of Writing a Cause and Effect Essay

Choose an event or a phenomenon to analyze. If you have the ability to choose the topic by yourself, decide whether you want to write about causes of some events, about effects, or to combine both. In case the topic is already given to you, you should clearly understand whether you are required to write about causes or effects. These two issues should be distinguished. Remember, causes are the answers to the question, "Why did this happen?" while effects can be understood after asking yourself, "What happened because of this?" (Writing Cause and Effect Essay, 2012).

Create an introduction that lets readers understand the general purpose of your cause and effect essay. The main points should be sketched in this part (usually in the thesis statement).

Write your thesis statement. Do not forget that this sentence is the most meaningful in the whole paper, which is why you should give this stage enough attention. List the causes and/or effects, as it will give your reader a view of the situation. Also, highlight whether you will discuss causes, effects, or both in the statement, and do not be afraid to use the terms "cause" and "effect."

Create the body of your essay. Adhere to a clear structure for the essay, do not forget to explain every idea (cause or effect), and find supporting ideas. The paragraphs, at the same time, can be organized in one of the following ways (Cause and Effect Essay, 2015):

- *Chronological.* The causes or effects are mentioned in the order in which events occurred.

- *Order of importance.* You list your points from the most important to the least or in reverse order.

Use appropriate transitions. As it was already mentioned, a cause and effect essay is based on the fundamental law of the nature and logic of thinking, therefore each idea should be properly connected to another one. The useful words and phrases will be listed in the next section of this guide (Guidelines and Tightening Your Essay).

Make a conclusion. Include not just the summary of the whole paper, paraphrasing the thesis statement, but explain why this analysis was important. Explain what the practical application or possible solution is to the problem.

Guidelines and Tightening Your Essay

From the previous section of this guide, you know that the process of creating a cause and effect essay starts similarly to other types of essays with the choice of what to write about. Below you can find a list of good topic examples for essays which concentrates on the causes of some issue, on the effects, and one topic that covers both.

Good Topic Examples

1. Does attending institutions of higher education cause people to have better marriages?

2. Why has the poverty level in the United States increased in the twenty-first century?

3. What are the causes of the rapid rise in overweight and obese young adults in the United States in the last twenty years?

4. Why did Google become the most popular search tool?

5. What are the main causes of American students having worse results on international tests in comparison to student from other countries?

6. Discuss the causes of illegal immigration.

7. Using technology in classrooms is the cause of better student learning. Do you agree with this statement?

8. Imagine that a government decided to introduce a policy similar to China's one-child policy. What are the possible consequences for family relationships?

9. Choose a non-profit organization and define social problems they address. What effect does the organization have on these problems?

10. Think how climate changes may affect the spread of infectious diseases in the modern world.

11. What are positive and negative impacts of video games on teenagers?

12. Think about students who have been labeled as "gifted" or "talented." Does it have any effects? Prove your position.

13. What are the outcomes of war with terrorists and in which way does it affect civilians?

14. What would the possible social effects be if everyone on the planet had the same level of prosperity?

15. Why do some people appeal to non-western medicine, and what are the consequences of their decision?

Useful Tips for Cause and Effect Essay Writing

Your task is not just to name the causes or effects of a phenomenon (action, event), which sometimes is called a trigger, but to show the logical connection between one issue and others (causes and outcomes) (Sahaj, 2015).

If you are limited to particular time frames or there are restrictions on the number of pages, concentrate only on the primary causes and effects. You can mention some minor points; however, do not go deep in their study. It will be a waste of time to speak about unlikely events. However, the "domino" type of structure may be named an exception as it requires finding a logical connection between several uncorrelated facts.

Do not forget to define the relations between the trigger and observed issues (Sahaj, 2015). In other words, you should state in the introduction whether you will be writing about causes of the phenomenon or about the effect it has. Some useful phrases will be: "It seems that the cause was the following…" or "The evidence may indicate that the main effect will be…" and "Available evidence suggests the following list of causes…"

Do not be afraid to use supporting materials. Remember, every piece of material is a good tool to prove your position. The experts recommend to define terms, claim some well-known facts, and even use personal observations to make your arguments sound more significant.

Useful Transition Words and Phrases

It was already highlighted that the correct presentation of thoughts and ideas is the primary condition for a successful cause and effect essay. In the table below you can find phrases and words that will help you to master your writing.

Transitions to Show the Cause Relation

in the event that	for fear that
granted (that)	in order to
as / so long as	seeing / being that
on (the) condition (that)	If… then, unless
for the purpose of	because of, as, since, while, lest
with this intention	in case, provided that, so as to, owing
with this in mind	to, inasmuch as, due to

Transitions to Show the Effect Relation

as a result	thus
under those circumstances	because the
in that case	then
for this reason	hence
in effect	consequently
for	therefore

thereupon   accordingly

forthwith   henceforth

This list is only a portion of the phrases that you can use, so do not forget to seize the opportunity while showing the example and while creating the conclusion.

Mistakes to Avoid While Writing a Cause and Effect Essay

General Mistakes in Thesis Statements for Cause and Effect Essays

1. Using an interrogative form for a thesis statement. You might have already noticed that the topics for cause and effect essays are often formulated in the form of a question. Therefore, students often forget to rewrite a thesis to sound like a statement (not a question). Remember, the main purpose of the thesis is to express your opinion. If your approach to the issue is too philosophical and there is not a clear position, your essay will lose the meaning of the argumentation and turn into abstract reflections that have not found the answer. Leave the hesitation and be assured but not too radical.

2. Having too long thesis. Remember, an important criterion is the adherence to the basic canons. A thesis by its definition is capacious, but is not a long statement. Distinguish the conclusion from the arguments (within the sentence) and do not paint the thesis on the whole sheet.

3. Uncertainty. Do not use the thesis for further polemics — the reader should easily trace the chain of your thought and its ending. The uncertainty of the thesis raises only additional questions and gives the impression that you simply decided not to bring your thoughts to the end.

Other Common Mistakes While Writing a Cause and Effect Essay

1. Listing out the causes and/or effects before mentioning the purpose of the whole paper and the trigger (Klacsanzky, 2014).

2. Emphasizing quantity over quality. Students often make attempts to find as many causes and effects as possible without discussing each of them in sufficient volume.

3. Paying excessive attention to the details of one single cause and/or effect.

12

4. Ignoring the stage of explaining the connection between the trigger and points (reasons or outcomes).

5. Choosing one extraordinary topic and having problems with evidence (Klacsanzky, 2014).

6. Repeating the same ideas. Do not develop the same idea in two paragraphs (this contradicts the basic condition — separation). Remember, a new paragraph is a new argument.

7. Presenting extra information. Make sure that the sentences are directly related to the main topic. Even if you have an irresistible desire to write an incredibly interesting fact, reread it several times and think on it — maybe it is better to use it as a hook?

8. Being inconsistent. If in the one paragraph you use a link with another reason, make sure that this reason was described above. Do not confuse the logical connection, running ahead.

Cause and Effect Essay Writing Checklist

- Does the topic include a cause and effect relationship?

- Does the essay have a focus on causes, effects, or both? Is there a clear indication of this information?

- Does the thesis statement clearly identify the focus of the essay? Is the thesis statement free from typical mistakes?

- Did you consider all suitable causes or effects? Is there something you have forgotten or, on the contrary, some ideas that should be omitted? Were any irrelevant causes or effects included?

- Is the logical chain maintained? Is the chosen order of arranging causes and effects the most effective one?

- Did you use enough transitions? Were all of them used properly?

- Do you explain each cause and effect clearly and convincingly? Are there additional examples or details needed?

- Did you summarize all of the ideas in the conclusion? Did you prove the cause and effect connection between the trigger and points? Did you propose some solutions?

References

Cause and Effect Essay. (2015). In *Essay Info Writing Guides*. Retrieved from

    http://essayinfo.com/essays/cause_and_effect_essay.php

How to Write a Cause and Effect Essay on Any Topic. (n.d.). In *School Works*. Retrieved from

    http://www.scoolwork.com/EssayWritingGuide/how_to_write_cause_effect_essay_on_any

    _topic.aspx

Jennifer, C. (2014). How to Write a Cause and Effect Essay That Gets You an A+. In *Udemy Blog*.

    Retrieved from https://blog.udemy.com/how-to-write-a-cause-and-effect-essay/

Klacsanzky, N. (2014). How Not to Write Cause and Effect Essays. In *Academic Help*. Retrieved

    https://academichelp.net/blog/bad-cause-effect-essays.html

Sahaj, B. (2015). 5 Rules for Writing Cause and Effect Essays. In *Academic Help*. Retrieved from

    https://academichelp.net/blog/cause-effect-essays-writing-rules.html

Writing a Cause and Effect. (2012). In *Academic Help*. Retrieved from

    https://academichelp.net/academic-assignments/essay/write-cause-and-effect-essay.html

Sample 1. The Effects of Online Dating

In our time, the communication between men and women gradually conquered the sphere of information technologies. In the virtual world, it is often possible to make not only familiar relations, but also the development of relationships, which are called online dating and virtual love. However, couples that communicate virtually need to keep in mind the shortcomings of such a relationship, as poor communication and lack of commitment are due to a lack of emotional intimacy and specificity from Internet communication.

Currently, it is extremely easy to start relationships via the Internet because they are very easy to finish. There is no need to worry about how a person looks, what impression it creates. There is a charming illusion of a full emotional life, devoid of the inevitable shortcomings and the difficulties that are brought by real communication. However, the relationships that we are building in real life always require significant mental work on their creation, maintenance and commitment. Internet dating almost does not require an emotional connection. If something goes wrong, a partner just puts this contact to the black list. Besides, it is also possible to block the ability to send messages, change the address of an e-mailbox, and start everything again. The ease of creating contacts disaccustoms people to invest efforts in the maintenance of relations and creation of partnership. The result is numerous short and empty virtual relationships, fear of creating real relationships, the desire to blunt the feeling of loneliness, and more new virtual novels again and again.

Furthermore, the image of the other person created from the Internet communication is completely devoid of reality. People fill it with their fantasies, latent desires, unmet needs, and willingness to believe that people on the other side of the monitor are ideal for everything. During the communication with a virtual companion, most people indeed believe that they communicate with a man or women who suits them perfectly, and thereby understands them, and always listens attentively. However, actual communication takes place in one direction, and people communicate with the image of the person that they have developed. In that case, the content of the replicas do

15

not matter, since everything said will be attributed to a fictitious interlocutor image and endowed with the proper sense. Following further, due to monosyllabic online replicas and constant use of so-called emoticons, there is an influence on the development of communicative abilities which is rather negative (Cantoni, 2015). In some cases, when a person has a contact in real life, it becomes hard to find words or behave well, and the social deconditioning develops which provides an adverse effect on the communication between people.

Finally, one day, there will be a desire to meet with a virtual partner for real, and here it will turn out that the created image is unlikely to correspond to reality because of complex problems of such relations (Davis, 2014). Usually, disappointment follows after that, and sometimes even depression.

To sum up, living in a fantasy world seems great, but it is impossible to prolong the illusion infinitely for the virtual couples. The Internet provides great opportunities for the development of human relations, but the evidence suggests that it is not related to solid romantic relationships. The system of values, commitment, responsibility and the ability to establish a connection are significantly altered during online dating, which can provide painful consequences for the personal lives of people.

References

Cantoni, L. (2015). *Communication and Technology* (1st ed.). Berlin/Boston, Germany: De GruyterMouton.

Davis, L. (2014). *Love at First Click* (1st ed.). New York: Atria Books.

Sample 2. The Causes and Effects of Playing Candy Crush

Candy Crush Saga is on the top of the charts of the most profitable applications thanks to several key features. The game is very accessible because people can play the game both online and offline and it is free. The graphics and sound in the game are excellent and extremely attractive. However, the analysis of this game showed that the main secret of the success of *Candy Crush* is its control over unconscious processes in people's minds.

The primary peculiarity of this type of game is simple mechanics. The central task of the player is to make a combination of three identical objects, namely colorful candies, which are randomly located on the playing field, and to form a variety of combos to earn more points. The rules are so simple that the learning process is almost unconscious. Even at high levels, it is possible to play without significant mental effort. For instance, studies proved that our brains prefer simple strategies to complicated analytical thinking whenever possible (Kahneman, 2011). Therefore, the developers simplified the gameplay, but at the same time, did not sacrifice fun, and it is another key to success but also an obvious negative influence on people's critical thinking, as the game do not develop any relevant skills and qualities.

The creator of the game, King Digital Entertainment, offers its games for free which also motivates people to play. However, the company earns money by selling virtual goods. In the case of *Candy Crush Saga*, it is the additional moves and a variety of bonuses. The most expensive purchase that a player can make is $39.99. However, in fact, most of the purchases in the game are purchases of additional moves and lives that cost $0.99. It is incredible, but this system of "pay to continue" brings the company $633,000 every day (Dickey, 2013). Therefore, this game also makes people extremely venturesome and pushes them to buy cheap things which make a significant sum of money only later.

Another cause to play the game is that it allows a player to demonstrate personal achievements, and players are looking for cooperation, promising a mutual benefit, or social gestures in the form of a partnership or investment. These issues are important for human

17

socialization. It is known that motivation through rewards represents a feature of games that are addictive. It is not surprising that the player is indeed motivated by the rewards like social recognition through success, and rewards like superpowers during the game.

Finally, players have only five lives, and once they run out, they have to wait half an hour for another attempt. However, these limits do not irritate the player — they make *Candy Crush Saga* more attractive, as the gameplay is not boring. The issue of "deficiency" or "shortage" is one of the six principles of influence identified by psychologist Robert Cialdini. It means that a man has a natural desire for things that are simply not enough (Cialdini, 2007). *Candy Crush Saga* skillfully uses this principle. It is available only for a restricted period, so it will be more attractive than something that is available without any problems. As a consequence, players caught by this trick spend hours of their free time without realizing the effect of dependence.

To sum up, despite the fact that the casual gaming world of this game does not possess any of the properties of developing games like puzzles or useful mechanics, millions of people around the world every day play this game for hours due to psychological tricks. Eventually, playing this game can also lead to addictive issues, the lack of critical thinking, and problems of venturesome people.

References

Cialdini, R. (2007). *Influence* (1st ed.). New York: Collins.

Dickey, M. (2013). Insanely Popular Game Candy Crush Saga Is Bringing in an Estimated $633,000 a Day. *Business Insider*. Retrieved from http://www.businessinsider.com/candy-crush-saga-daily-revenue-2013-7

Kahneman, D. (2011). *Thinking, Fast and Slow* (1st ed.). Farrar, Straus and Giroux.

Chapter 2. Critical Essay Writing Guide

It is easy to predict your thoughts about this type of essay, which seems to be one of the easiest tasks you have ever faced. They say, it is always simple to critique work of other people than creating your own. However, in the case of a critical essay, you should do both tasks and do it perfectly. So, this guide will be helpful in your aspirations to have a well-written critical essay.

What's So Special About a Critical Essay?

The sense of a critical essay (sometimes called critical analysis) can be understood from the name — to write a critical review of a research paper, book, film, or painting. Students in any field, no matter if it is science or the arts, are required to have an analytical mind, so they are often asked to write this type of essay. If you are not a student or have not yet been assigned to write the critical essay, I am sure that you have at least general knowledge about these reviews and analyses, even though they are often not academic types of papers. Almost everyone has read at least once some of them such as reviews of books or movies. Nevertheless, returning the discussion back to academic papers, it can be noticed that students associate the concept of a critical essay with the negative

19

opinion about the creator and their creation. To overcome this fallacy, the essence of critical analysis will be studied in more detail.

What Is a Critical Analysis?

The critical analysis definition may be formulated as "an academic paper designed to understand a certain written work" (How to Write a Critical Analysis Essay, 2015). We cannot say that the previous assumption is totally false, rather it is only a part of the truth. To speak more literally, the adjective "critical" should be replaced by the term "evaluative" and be perceived both in positive and negative meaning.

Another important point you should be familiar with is the level of personalization laid into the critical essay. Essays of such type are subjective, considering the task that usually stands behind them — to provide personal opinions. This, of course, does not mean that it is enough to say, "This story or book was bad (the author is not talented) because I did not like this piece of art or science." The numerous sources devoted to advice on writing critical essays insist that students should take two steps — critical reading and critical writing. Now, let us have a closer look at the issue of creating the essay.

How to Write a Critical Analysis?

The first stage in a critical path analysis is critical reading, which assumes that, in parallel with reading, there is an analysis of the author's purpose, his or her arguments, and the means used. Ideally, you are recommended to take notes and refer to credible sources when facing something you lack the competency to discuss. Only after such critical reading of texts, or watching films or observing sculptures, can you start writing a critical essay. Here the basic point is to write, keeping in mind the defined author's purpose and whether it was achieved.

Unconditionally, this knowledge is still not enough to write an excellent work so we will review the critical essay critically.

Critical Essay Writing Structure

The best way to understand something is to look inside to understand how it works. In case of a critical essay, we will firstly look at the skeleton of the paper — it's outline. Below you will find the most common example for a critical essay, which still can be transformed by your desire or in case you will be given some additional requirements.

You will notice that the structure for a critical essay is slightly different from the traditional five-paragraph structure. Even still, three parts, including an introduction with a thesis statement, the body, and conclusion should be followed.

Background information. This is the obligatory part where you state the purpose of your work, mentioning the topic and sometimes why you decided to choose this topic. Although the information should be briefly spelled out, all important details should be included to define some basis of the future evaluation.

Information about the work. The main feature of a critical essay is an absence of intrigue; in other words, from the very beginning you must indicate the basic information about the subject of your critical evaluation, such as title, author, publication information, statement of topic, and purpose (How to Write a Critical Analysis Essay, 2015).

Even though previously it was mentioned that the critical essay has some peculiarities of structure, it still should contain a thesis statement indicating your main reaction to the work.

Summary. In fact, this part marks the beginning of the main body of the essay if we want to draw parallels with a more traditional perception of essay structuring. The summary, without a doubt, can be named as a fundamental part of the critical analysis. This part proves that you have completed at least part of the task — you have read or seen or listened to the subject. Furthermore, it proves that you considered and analyzed the received information.

Interpretation. Finally the part for the sake of which everything was started — your personal subjective interpretation. "It should be based on your experiences, and honest opinions be it negative or positive" (How to Write a Critical Analysis Essay, 2015). These words should be your credo while you will write your paper. Based on your experience, proficiency, and personality, the evaluation will be a unique one. Possible themes that may be addressed are the organization of the work, style of the work, the meaning pledged in work, and the methods and effectiveness of appealing to a particular audience.

Conclusion. Summarize all of your ideas; however, check if this part matches the introduction regarding ideas and arguments as well as the general tone of the essay.

As already mentioned, this outline serves as a good support element for creating your critical essay, yet do not be afraid to experiment and create your subjective style and structure of analysis.

Stages of Writing a Critical Essay

1. Start with the choice! This can be named the most important stage (unless, of course, you weren't given the right to choose). Think about a text, article, film, piece of music, or play that you want to analyze from a critical point. Be sure that you are totally informed about it before you start writing. This means that you should be familiar with the original, and not just some reviews or critical essays of others.

2. Begin the critical reading. Pay attention so that in this case reading is used in a much wider context determined by the object of analysis (observation in case you want to discuss a film, or listening when we are talking about a song).

3. Focus on annotation. Note moments that cause you to be concerned or to take a critical look, and include some questions that arise in the process of reading. Think about your position and arguments.

4. Start the preparation of future references. Search some relevant and credible materials to make your arguments sound more convincing. Do not forget that all articles, books and online materials comply if they are scholarly and not popular.

5. Write the body. Despite the fact that it sounds strange, the majority of authors working with critical essay writing recommend to start with the main and the most responsible part (Writing

a Critical Essay, 2012). Do not forget that each paragraph must correspond with one single point for or against the thesis (the latter is used in case you want to show an opposite view).

6. Focus on summarizing for the conclusion. As you can see, the stranger elements have not concluded in the previous step, but this is true — before you write the introduction, it is better to create a conclusion that sums up all of the points and the argument.

7. Now begin writing the actual introduction. The introduction is written last to make sure that it will cover all of what you have said throughout the text.

8. Work on the final step. This includes reading, correction, editing, and checking one more time, and then your critical essay is done!

Guidelines and Tightening Your Essay

Along with the decision about the subject of the future essay and the topic in general, one more choice should be made — to use a *critical style* (Writing a Critical Essay, 2012). Here are three different methods of the critical style.

The claim and evidence. While using this style, the author should make a number of claims and support each of them with evidence. In this case, evidence would be citations, examples, testimony from the text, and other materials that will be properly cited and used as references.

The new information method. In this critical style, after the presentation of information, the author provides his or her new ideas and thoughts, fresh research or possible topics for further exploration and discussion.

Examination and exploration. This style is aimed at finding the details and thinking (exploration) of motivations, aspirations of the author and meanings that can be found in the text, piece of literature, or art.

Good Topic Examples

Before listing the examples of topics that may inspire you to create the perfect critical essay, some words about features of topics in the critical essay should be told. In fact, the title that represents the topic in essays of a critical nature consists of two parts. The first reflects the object you have chosen — the book, article, or picture. The second part refers to the theme revealed in the object of analysis. The refinement is needed because objects are not univariate and usually cover several topics which differ in significance. Therefore, you have an opportunity to limit your future paper by eliminating all unnecessary topics and concentrating on one.

Now, you can check this example list of good topics to choose while writing a critical essay:

1. The place of women in Nathaniel Hawthorne's literature.

2. The concepts of families in Ancient Greek literature.

3. The innocence and the evil in Harper Lee's *To Kill a Mockingbird*.

4. The role of Willy Loman in Arthur Miller's play *Death of a Salesman*.

5. "True love" in Jane Austen's *Pride and Prejudice*.

6. The "real monster" of Mary W. Shelley's *Frankenstein*.

7. The hidden meaning in the paintings of René Magritte.

8. Pop-up ads in Web advertising.

9. Suicide in the works of Émile Durkheim.

10. Mass media liberal bias.

11. Eyewitness memory to recall a crime is infallible.

12. Economic development since 1950.

13. Lost Generation: cause and benefits.

14. United Nations and the environment.

15. Criticizing Donald Trump's inauguration speech.

Useful Tips for Writing a Critical Essay

Below, you will find a list with practical tips on writing a critical essay. These recommendations are given by writers who have vast experience in completing essays.

- Critical thinking is essential for people in modern life, so demonstrate your critical writing skills by exploring academic theories, discussing arguments, and providing evidence.

- Along with analyzing the meaning of the reading itself, do not forget to evaluate the data that was used regarding reliability and explications (of course if it is possible) (Critical Essay, n.d.).

- Even though a critical essay is subjective writing, your emphasis should be made not on feelings and groundless criticism, but on the structure, facts, language, and meanings.

- Find the balance between analysis and the details to demonstrate that you have examined the objective and theme thoroughly.

- A good way to create the basis of the interpretation is to consider how the methods used by the author while writing the work influenced the general meaning of the text.

- Do not be afraid of using philosophical notions — for example, logic, deduction, and rhetorical tools (ethos, pathos, logos). Use persuasive techniques to prove the author's position or, on the contrary, to argue the lack of value in the text.

- It is important to define criticism properly — when we are talking about academic writing, to criticize means to analyze, and not just saying that it is wrong or bad.

- At the stage of formulating a topic, do not try to write about everything; remember the duality of topics and narrow it for your taste.

- Focus on the aspects that you are interested in or aware of — it will simplify your work.

- Remember that the essay should focus on the analysis, not on your personality, so avoid statements that point to you, including "I think," "to my mind," and "in my opinion."

- If you feel that you do not have a full understanding of the above components of the work after the first reading, read it again, but this time take these components into account before proceeding with the analysis.

- Check to see if, instead of a critical analysis, you start to just give the presentation of the work.

Mistakes to Avoid While Writing a Critical Essay

While working on critical essays, students often make mistakes which hinder them from creating A-level papers. In this section, you will find the most common mistakes and explanations on how to avoid them.

- The biggest mistake with which even the most experienced writers are faced with is the fear of a blank list. You do not know what to write first, and end up making a big mistake — you stop trying to write. Remember, it does not matter where you start: most importantly, do not stop writing and do not worry about style and spelling.

- Using strong language or repetition: it will be enough to support the claims with evidence without excessive emotions.

- Appealing to the current fashion in your thoughts. Note that an effective critical essay should address the reader's sentiments and logical thoughts.

- Making points that do not reveal your opinion fully. However, remember that even such statements should be argumentative enough.

- Using informal language while writing academic papers. In spite of the fact that a critical essay is a subjective type of paper, the style of language should be argumentative and professional enough to defend the position properly.

- Omitting direct quotes from the original text and relevant papers. The main mistake that accompanies this one is the use of sources that are unreliable and do not meet the criteria of being up-to-date.

- Using too many negative sentences. You should remember that a critical essay does not equate to a negatively colored essay — it can be as positive as any other type of essay writing.

- Replacing the thesis and arguments with facts, data, and other sources of evidence.

- Writing a weak thesis statement that only states a broad opinion. For example, "*The Great Gatsby* is a great example of American literature," is weak, while "*The Great Gatsby* captures the essence of America's Jazz Age in its decadence, materialism, and ultimately, its tragic emptiness," emphasizes the main idea of the future paper and is specific enough.

- Using new material in the conclusion is a common mistake that writers should try to avoid.

Now that you have become acquainted with the definition of the critical essay and have learned about structure, tips for writing, and what mistakes to avoid, you can check out your essay once again to be sure that it will be the best it can be and deserves an excellent grade.

Critical Essay Writing Checklist

- Is there an introduction with an attention getter that grabs the interest of the audience? Is the thesis statement clearly stated and described as well?

- Are the main points reflected by the topic sentences supported with concrete and detailed examples? Do the main points relate to the thesis directly?

- Are topic sentences clear and do all of them relate to the thesis? Do the rest of the parts of the body paragraphs support each of the topic sentences? Is there enough evidence, which means that there is no need for additional examples or details?

- Do you think the examples you have used are the best? What are the weaknesses of your examples? Are there any ambiguities?

- What are the strengths and weaknesses of your arguments? Are the arguments clear?

- Is there logic in the presentation of ideas throughout the whole paper? Are transitions used appropriately? Do they vary with structure? Are they not limited to their usage only in the topic sentence?

- Is this essay your analysis, your interpretation, and your presentation of the ability to think critically? Check the balance between descriptive and critical elements of writing. Do not forget that a critical essay is not a retelling of a book.

- Does the conclusion make sense? Does the conclusion have a distinct ending rather than simply an abrupt stop?

- Is your critical essay free from wordiness, clichés, and gender or race biased language? Does the text contain an appropriate vocabulary, and use active instead of passive voice?

In conclusion, it is worth noting that in any essay people try to see the image of the person who wrote it. Remember this idea and do not be afraid to be overly critical (if you criticize in fact) or too soft (as in academic writing, there is also positive criticism), just present your own thoughts.

References

Critical essay. (n.d.). In *Essay Writing Tips*. Retrieved from

http://www.essay-writing-tips.com/types-of-essays/critical-essay.html

How to Write a Critical Analysis Essay. (2015). In *EssayPro*. Retrieved from

https://essaypro.com/blog/critical-analysis-essay/

Writing a Critical Essay. (2012). In *Academic Help*. Retrieved from

https://academichelp.net/academic-assignments/essay/write-critical-essay.html

Sample 1. Genetically Modified Foods

Some people consider genetically modified foods an excellent alternative; however, there are still many controversies. The danger of these products has not been proven, while there are fervent argues that such food causes severe changes to the digestive system and weakening of the immune system. In any case, there is an urgent necessity to feed a growing population on a limited resource, and the solution has not been found yet.

A healthy way of living, along with vegetarianism, is becoming more mainstream, reducing consumption of genetically modified foods because these products may affect the immune system through the intestinal microflora, to provoke cancer, and disrupt metabolism (Wunderlich, 2015). Overall, 40% of consumers report avoiding GMOs in their diet, 71% of whom were worried about health repercussions and 48% wanting to know "exactly what goes into the food [they] eat" (Wunderlich, 2015). Organic products can be viewed as a better alternative, and they do not contain genetically modified organisms (GMOs). In addition to the lack of harmful substances, organic products are distinguished by their flavor and higher nutritional properties. In comparison to GM meat, organic meat is an exceptional source of healthy protein and abundant amino acids. The recent empirical survey based on animal feeding has shown that "GM foods have toxic effects, including abnormal changes in organs, immune system disturbances, accelerated aging, and changes in gene expression" (Wunderlich, 2015). Consequently, the same effects occur with a human if tracing the food chain. On this basis, one can only assume the possible effects that could influence human's body after lasting GM food administration.

Therefore, although biotech foods are better for quantitative measurement, organic foods are more digestible, tasty and healthy and a human needs not so much of them to be full. There are still two convincing arguments for GM products development. Firstly, vegetables cultivated in such a way have the perfect appearance and are unexposed to pests, which allows farmers to save larger areas of crops. GMO products are stored for a long time, unnaturally long in any storage conditions.

To contradict the "beneficial" impact that a GMO has on the feeding issue, another alternative can be found. Scientists are seeking new approaches and succeed, claiming that yet one of the best targets for improving this situation is engineering plants to increase their photosynthetic activity. According to this principle, people could "grow more food on less land" that will "keep up the human population causing less damage than GM feeding" (Bonham, 2015).

Norman Borlaug, the winner of the Nobel Prize for his work in "curbing world hunger through The Green Revolution," is convinced that "GMOs can feed the planet" (Wyly, 2012). From the economical point of view, without GMO technology, it would be tough to feed the planet and unthinkable for the further development of humanity as a species. However, if people could think more globally, there is no problem of limited resources, but it is rather a question of the current state of resource allocation. The matter is that the lion's share of the production goes to biofuels and other forms of energy.

Consequently, genetic engineering can help protect nature, if used wisely. However, on the current stage, people do not have enough information about this issue to be sure that GM products will save the planet and not degrade it.

References

Wunderlich, S., & Gatto, K. A. (2015). Consumer Perception of Genetically Modified Organisms and Sources of Information. *Advances in Nutrition: An International Review Journal*, 6(6), 842851. doi:10.3945/an.115.008870

Bonham, K. (2015, March 31). GMOs Are Still the Best Bet for Feeding the World. Retrieved from https://blogs.scientificamerican.com/food-matters/gmos-are-still-the-bestbet-for-feeding-the-world/

Wyly, C. (n.d.). The Future of Food Series: Exponential Solutions to Transforming Our Food System. Retrieved from http://www.huffingtonpost.com/christiana-wyly/urbanfarming-_b_2272249.html

Sample 2. The Blair Witch Project

The film *The Blair Witch Project* is about students who went to the Black Hills wood to create a documentary about the local legend of Blair Witch, who torments and kills everyone who comes into her territory. This legend addresses an ancient curse, evil artifacts and ritual murders of children. The students were lost several hours after they entered Black Hills. The film shows terrible events that began and everything that happened was filmed on the camera of one of the heroes. Since then, nobody has seen the documentary lovers, until a year later, when people found captured materials. This film was a revolution in the genre, and due to its documentary style, it maximizes the effect of the presence of the viewer and horror experience as well.

The Blair Witch Project is an experimental film that marked the beginning of a new genre, namely "found footage." This is horror direction, in which film allegedly was found by someone, and it is demonstrated to the viewer without qualitative camera work, which recreates the nearly real-life experience. In general, film and the objective reality of its interpenetration were subjected to controversy since the dawn of cinema. Concerning featured film, it is primarily about the limits of realism. The horror film genre, throughout its narrative, sought to ensure the most realistic events.

All key features of found footage can be identified as the desire to convey the authenticity of the event, its reality, and a high probability that it can happen to anyone. The authors use the style of a documentary to achieve the chosen objectives, recognizing that viewers are accustomed to perceiving such information in the framework of real events. This habit is triggered on the reflex level and enhances viewers participation. In most cases, the audience is well aware that they face a fictional story, but at the same time, they are inadvertently involved in the game due to the chosen form of the show.

In *The Blair Witch Project*, the viewer will not see any killings, but we know that they happened. Also, viewers can not see the witch herself, and it is impossible to judge whether she existed. In this case, the viewer additionally avoids the frustration regarding the appearance of the antagonist, according to the paradox of Stephen King, namely that what lies behind the door or at the top of the stairs will never scare us as well as the staircase or door itself (King, 1981). It is also symbolic that *The Blair Witch Project* uses a technique that Freud in his article "Uncanny" calls the unintended return. It is a return to childhood's fears which increases the psychological impact on the person and results in a sense of helplessness (Freud, 1919). In the film, there is a children's fear of getting lost in the forest, combined with the legend of the witch.

Thus, the secret of success of the found footage genre is the focus on the maximum inclusion of the viewer in the created reality. For this aim, found footage skillfully mimics a chronicle and uses the conventions of documentary and amateur filming. Eventually, the audience is scared because it seems that the events occurred with their direct participation.

References

Freud, S. (1919). The 'Uncanny'. The Standard Edition of the Complete Psychology.

King, S. (1981). *Stephen King's Danse Macabre* (1st ed.). New York: Everest House.

Chapter 3. Deductive Essay Writing Guide

Every person who has heard about the great detective Sherlock Holmes is familiar with his well-known deductive method. "The deductive method is useful in a detective job," you may say, "but what is a deductive essay and how does it connect to the deduction at all?" This section is aimed at helping you to understand and complete the task of writing a high-quality deductive essay.

What's So Special About a Deductive Essay?

If you are faced with writing a deductive essay, the conclusion that can be made with high probability is the fact that you are a student. An essay based on deductive reasoning is a tool for evaluating the knowledge of students as well as a method of encouraging students' logical thinking, and improving their skills of finding information and structuring it. The deductive essay is a type of academic writing that shows the author's ability to use reasonable assumptions to come to a logical conclusion on a variety of topics.

33

The key characteristics of an excellent deductive essay are clarity and focus. This means that the particular idea or point of view will be weak without clear support. In other words, each paragraph should focus on a single aspect or point with the use of details and examples to lead to a specific conclusion.

In this type of essay, the organization of paragraphs is highly important. In fact, the structure (which will be discussed in detail below) reflects the traditional construction of deductive reasoning — from general to specific. Of course, the proposed one is the most simple and general explanation of the nature of the deductive approach (to start from the most general knowledge to the specific facts). Speaking more academically, this concept is the conviction that a person can give a reasonable assumption to the specific situation in the case of having enough clues or descriptions of circumstances — in other words, information about the subject (Deductive Essay, n. d.). In fact, every student is familiar with deductive reasoning from the college course of logic where the conclusion on the basis of two statements should be proposed. To make it more clear, let's take a look at an example:

Statement1: *All cats are animals.*

Statement2: *A kitty is a cat.*

Conclusion: *A kitty is an animal.*

This exercise is quite simple, but it gives the opportunity to understand the logic behind deductive reasoning.

Without a doubt, you still can have a feeling that writing deductive essays goes beyond your capabilities. I want to reassure you — there is no need to be afraid if you think that you do not have a deductive style of thinking. To follow this style of essay just means that within your paper you take identified factors, compare them with the familiar or general knowledge, and add them in the form of a conclusion. These requirements are reflected in the structure of the deductive essay, which consists of a premise, evidence, and a conclusion (How to Write a Deductive Essay?, n.d.). In our example, Statement 1 was a premise, while evidence is described by the second sentence. That is why using such analogy, you will be able to write an excellent deductive essay.

Deductive Essay Writing Structure

Although the previous part of this guide may be a little bit confusing, you should not panic — in general, the deductive essay has a common structure, with introduction, body, and conclusion paragraphs.

Introduction — premise

As always, the first part introduces the topic to the readers, states the main ideas and thesis of the paper, and serves the main purpose to attract attention.

What are the specifics? The first part also provides the set of premises — facts, ideas, clues, and information from common knowledge that in the result will help to arrive at a conclusion.

Remember! There can be more than one premise for one argument, so you should list them all. In addition, there is the thought that in a deductive essay, the author can avoid the typical thesis statements, as in the majority of cases, the thesis will be the conclusion (How to Write a Deductive Essay? n. d.).

Body — evidence

This part focuses on the pieces of evidence that can be defined as described and analyzed facts or pieces of information which are determined by the premises. Such collection of evidence is the proof on which the author can rely, such as personal experience, expert testimony, and statistics. However, do not forget that such pieces should seem logical for the audience as well as for your personal point of view.

What are the specifics? In the case of writing the body of the deductive essay, you are working not with the idea as a whole, but with its parts. This means that each paragraph should reflect a single part of the idea and be put together section by section. If you complete this task successfully, the body will be the part of the essay where the main idea is proven or expanded upon; therefore, the logic of deductive reasoning will be sustained (McMillan, 1984).

Remember! Do not overload your paper with pieces of evidence — usually, three paragraphs, each of which is devoted to a single idea, are enough to express thoughts and to prove the conclusion. One more piece of advice is to use several types of evidence. This means that one example from personal experience and one piece of evidence from a scientific article is better than two stories from everyday life.

Conclusion

Finally, the last part presents the conclusion formulated by taking into account the premises and evidence. This section shows the final step, where you arrive at a certain position after the entire analysis. Remember that the conclusion in a deductive essay, as in any other type, should be unambiguous and clearly formulated.

What are the specifics? The final paragraph of the essay on deductive reasoning should contain the thesis and the deductive conclusion.

Remember! This type of reasoning may have several potential conclusions, and this is a normal situation. However, it is important for a student to choose the one most logical and appropriate among the variety. Once again, it is essential to discuss the single conclusion, otherwise, the essay would lose focus and persuasive impact on the future readers.

Stages of Writing a Deductive Essay

Before proceeding directly to steps and sequences necessary for successful deductive essay writing, I want to draw your attention to the well-known fact that the quality of any essay depends on three interrelated components: including the used raw material, the quality of the available sources, and reasoning. This means that most of your attention should be paid to the quality (organization, argumentation) and quantity (academic articles, lectures, discussions, personal thoughts and experiences) of the selected sources as well as the degree of correlation with the thematic content of the future paper. Regarding this, the process of writing the essay can be divided into several stages: *thinking, planning, writing, checking, and correction*.

So, the first stage is *thinking*, which, in turn, starts with the choice of the topic. Of course, in the overwhelming majority of cases, you are limited by the requirements of the professor. In this case, you can focus on thinking about the information that should be used and the general concept of the future work. The essential point in such case is to understand the depth of knowledge needed to complete the task successfully.

The opposite case is a situation when you are limited only by the overall theme of the course or the type of essay. If you get stuck at this stage, which is the very beginning, do not despair, as it is a common reaction of students. You should look at the problem from a different angle (and of course do not forget to breathe). Just remember that if the topic is not given from the outside, you are free to choose anything you like: what concerns you personally, or something you are familiar with, or perhaps something socially significant. Returning to deductive essay writing, it should be noted that topics are often dualistic, so you can choose the position you like the most — it will help you to make the essay more meaningful and profound. After coping with this task, you can easily move to thinking about the sources and information that should be included. Please note that by the end of the stage of thinking, you should have in mind the central idea and the points that can be used to support it.

The next stage is *planning*, at the end of which you should have the completed outline. In fact, the outline of the paper is named by several authors as the skeleton of the future paper (McMillan, 1984). In this particular type of essay, the process of creating the outline can be divided into the preparation of the deductive outline and the complete text outline. The first represents the logical structure of the proof of the central idea. The creation of the second outline displays the traditional preparation to essay writing, where the structure of the future paper is composed.

The next stage, known as the *writing* stage, can be presented as the combination of two substages as well. These substages are different in terms of the final product. This means that at the end of the first step, the complete rough draft is created, and then after the polishing, the final version of the text is completed. The process of polishing, in the case of creating an essay with the use of deductive reasoning, concentrates on paragraph development and ensuring sentence variety.

After the full essay is ready, you start the process of **checking** for mistakes in both logic and grammar. Taking into account the fact that the second is more simple in execution, the greater attention in this guide, as well as your own during the writing process, should be made on checking the completion of the deductive structure of reasoning (it will be discussed later in the Useful Tips section).

Finally, the last step is *a correction* of the essay and a final check. In fact, this step is the easiest one, but do not forget the basic principle of checking an essay of any type — to read the final version several times. Just keep in mind that your paper should be easy to read and understand, and, of course, as a deductive type of paper, it should prove the central idea.

Guidelines and Tightening Your Essay

Now we are ready to know the useful tips that will help you complete the deductive essay writing assignment successfully.

Previously, we had already reviewed the importance of topic choice (in case it was not set to you). We have also prepared a list of good and bad topic examples which will come in handy, or at least orient the worthy direction of thinking.

Good Topic Examples

1. International immigrants and freedom.

2. Democracy versus communism.

3. Terrorism knows no borders.

4. The harm of the lie versus the harm of truth.

5. Is cloning morally accepted?

6. Is there any limit for knowledge?

7. Is it right to judge other people?

8. Traditional versus online education: what to choose?

9. Technology in the classroom.

10. Should the government be permitted to police the Internet?

11. Impact of global warming and current government policies.

12. Should nuclear stations be closed?

13. Nobody is perfect.

14. People are never ready for changes.

15. Is the nuclear family system better than the joint family system?

Here are some more ideas about writing in the form of deductive reasoning. Without a doubt, this part of the entire work will be the most challenging for the majority of readers. If you caught yourself thinking that you are now a part of this team, there is no reason for catastrophe. Just pay attention to this part of the guide!

It goes without saying that it is easier for us to understand unknown information explained by the use of familiar analogies. The best explanation of the deductive outline (the importance of which was stated above) was proposed by May Flewellen McMillan. In her book, it is stated that the outline of deductive reasoning can be imagined as a family tree. Each topic (A, B, C) in this case will be a single family with the unique style of living and physical or mental attributes. Such family units are related with each other and can be attributed to the particular branch on the tree, the latter representing the topics I, II, and III. Such greater topics, in fact, correlate with each other as all of them have the common ancestor, and it means that each of the I, II, and III topics proves the central idea (1984). You will agree that this explanation is much easier to read, thus the deductive reasoning outline will not be a serious problem anymore.

Useful Tips for Deductive Essay Writing

- To make your future deductive essay an A-level one, the essential part that should not be forgotten is the argument style.

- No less attention should be paid to the first sentences of each paragraph. In fact, there is a strong belief that deductive reasoning is a perfect choice if the audience is not likely to read the whole piece of writing. However, using the correct words for the first paragraph will allow the reader to scan the text and get the main idea (Fudge, 2015).

- It is a well-known fact that the introduction is an essential but often underrated part of the essay. In a deductive essay, the task is to propose the conclusion with the use of logical thinking, which is why the beginning should catch the attention of the potential readers, while the thesis should be clear and strong (McMillan, 1984).

- Use objective voice and stick with both outlines to produce the deductive arrangement and connected ideas.

- While writing the essay, the transitions (linking words, phrases, or sentences) should be placed at the beginning of the paragraph instead of at the end of the preceding (McMillan, 1984).

- Do not be afraid to shorten your essay if you feel that it is overloaded with information. Nevertheless, be very careful with the evidence, as the lack of support to the premise will have a negative impact on the deductive side of the essay (which is the basis for this type).

- Pay attention to the language. On the one hand, the vocabulary should be academical as the deductive essay is a formal type of writing. On the other hand, you need to focus on the audience, therefore the language must match the writing style. For example, it is not recommended to use complicated terminology if writing an essay on an everyday topic.

Mistakes to Avoid While Writing a Deductive Essay

Mistakes related to the topic. As you can see, deductive essays often propose to work with topics containing comparisons. Regarding this, the typical mistake is the confusion of several different types of essay writing. It can be paraphrasing: when you face a dual theme and there is no ability to specify it, there is no necessity for a description of each option separately and a comparison of them — you should only prove the specific issue. For example, if the topic is "democracy versus totalitarianism," you are not required to describe the similarities and differences of these political regimes. In your deductive essay, you should defend the point of why only one among them can exist in the contemporary world.

Mistakes in paragraphs. A common mistake of students is to follow the overall structure of the essay (when each paragraph represents a single evidence of the premise) ignoring the appropriate structure of each paragraph. Please note that each sentence in the paragraph should explain and expand the first claim (sentence).

Common mistakes to avoid in deductive essays:

- mixing premises with evidence;

- describing the different variants of conclusions;

- overloading the essay with excessive information;

- confusing inductive and deductive methods of reasoning.

Deductive Essay Writing Checklist

- Does the essay reveal the topic which was clarified with the use of deductive reasoning?

- Does the essay contain the premise, pieces of evidence that prove the central idea, and the conclusion that is followed from the reasoning?

- Will the logic be understandable for the potential audience?

- Does the essay contain enough evidence to verify the conclusion?

- Within each paragraph, have you moved from abstract to concrete ideas?

- Do the paragraphs together have unity and coherence?

- Is there variety in the type and length of sentences?

- Was the vocabulary used appropriately due to personal knowledge and for potential readers?

Answering all of these questions will help you ensure that your essay is great or will be such after the final polishing. Nevertheless, now you are ready to write the best essay with the use of deductive reasoning.

References

Deductive Essay. (n. d.). In *Essay Info Writing Guides*. Retrieved from

http://essayinfo.com/essays/deductive_essay.php

Fudge, T. (2015). Inductive vs. Deductive Writing. *Kaplan University Academic Support Center Blog*. Retrieved from https://kuwcnews.wordpress.com/2015/02/25/inductive-vs-deductive-writing/

How to Write a Deductive Essay? (n. d.). In *Write a Writing*. Retrieved from

http://www.writeawriting.com/essay/how-to-write-deductive-essay/

McMillan, M. F. (1984). *The Shortest Way to the Essay: Rhetorical Strategies*. Mercer University Press.

Sample 1. Does Pain and Sorrow Make One Stronger?

Some of the great thinkers developed the idea that difficulties can temper a person, and pain with sorrow, make one stronger. Moreover, some people adore the idea that the painful feelings of fear, uncertainty, and doubt only stimulate a strong personality to gain new knowledge. On the contrary, the evidence assumes that pain and sorrow make one weaker due to the harmful effect of these feelings.

To start with, it is important to determine what personality should be called a strong personality. According to Klingemann and Römmele (2002), strong characters are distinguished by emotional speech, a spontaneous expression of their emotions, directness of statements, and defense of their opinions. Also, the strength of the human spirit manifests itself in certain character traits like confidence. Strong people soberly assess their abilities, and they are confident to reach the goal. Another quality of this personality is the ability to build relationships with others. Strong people have a capacity to accept people as they are. Therefore, they can establish robust and profound friendly relations with colleagues, friends, relatives, and neighbors. Powerful people can even control others and determine their behavior. Therefore, it is possible to assume the following premises, namely, that pain and sorrow make people more confident, and that pain and sorrow make it easy to establish the relations.

Someone may argue that pain is the lesson of how to act in a similar future situation. On the contrary, each life experience is unique, and the popular expression of Heraclitus says: "No man ever steps in the same river twice, for it's not the same river and he's not the same man" (Sedley, 2003). It turns out that life is the road which is scattered with a variety of problems and not those which the person has already left behind, but entirely new. Failures and troubles drop a person back, and eventually, it seems tough to stay with a clear and sober mind. Moreover, for those who face pain and sorrow regularly, the situation is even worse because there appears a mental coding to the negative mood, and it becomes increasingly difficult to break out of a vicious circle. Thus, the depression develops, and the evidence shows that pain is one of the factors that can lead to

43

depression (Beck & Alford, 2014). Therefore, it is unlikely that confidence appears after a negative experience.

Furthermore, according to the scientists, people who have experienced a break in a relationship consider it as a traumatic event. It leads to psychological discomfort, frustration, humiliation and damage to self-esteem. However, the most relevant evidence on that issue is internal passiveness and an indifferent attitude to the construction of a new relationship (Berman & Turk, 1981). Despite the fact that people may suffer from loneliness, they will not attempt to find new relations since they are not ready for a new closeness. Thus, the negative features of pain and sorrow from the break of relations provoke a decline of social activity and prevent new relationships.

To sum up, it is impossible to consider pain and sorrow as the factors that can help a person to become stronger. The evidence shows that issues of grief and sorrow can provide a significant impact on the characteristics of a strong person. Therefore, depression, lack of confidence, and the fear of establishing relations do not correlate to the qualities of a strong personality.

References

Beck, A. & Alford, B. (2014). *Depression* (1st ed.). Philadelphia: University of Pennsylvania Press.

Berman, W., & Turk, D. (1981). Adaptation to Divorce: Problems and Coping Strategies. *Journal of Marriage and Family*, 43(1), 179-189. doi:10.2307/351428

Klingemann, H. & Römmele, A. (2002). *Public Information Campaigns & Opinion Research* (1st ed.). London: SAGE.

Sedley, D. (2003). *Plato's Cratylus* (1st ed.). Cambridge: Cambridge University Press.

Sample 2. Being in Fashion Does Not Mean Having Taste

The majority of people commonly believe that being in fashion is the most important factor influencing an individual sense of style. However, in the actual circumstances, everything is different. Today's world is rapidly developing, inventing new technologies and suggesting new ways of dressing, studying, traveling. Due to this, following fashion tendencies becomes merely impossible, as new colors, textiles and their combinations are being labeled as fashionable every day. In this way, fashion is a concept, the meaning of which is continually changing. In contradistinction from it, taste always remains the same. It is essential to draw the line between the taste and the fashion, teaching humans about the difference between these concepts and emphasizing the importance of personal style but not current fashion.

Some people believe that being fashionable means having exquisite taste. These people buy the most expensive accessories and clothes to make their looks impeccable, believing that they save themselves from unreasonable fashion-related judgments. However, wearing the clothes from the latest collections is not a marker of great taste, as people may combine the clothes in a terrible manner and look comical. In this way, how people wear the clothes is more important than what they wear. Unfortunately, the age of rapidly growing consumerism has significantly affected the people, making them confuse the concepts of taste and fashion, giving the preference to the latter.

The distinction between these two terms is based on the meaning of both. Cambridge Dictionary suggests the following definition of fashion: "a style that is popular at a particular time, especially in clothes, hair, make-up, etc." (2017) Accordingly, with the help of this definition, it becomes evident that fashion is imposed by other people—some authorities, designers and models, who struggle to invent something new and surprise their potential customers by extraordinary decisions. Furthermore, fashion is changeable and flexible, as it is popular only in a particular time. Paradoxically, the definition of taste is entirely different from the concept of fashion, as Cambridge Dictionary (2017) explains that the taste is "a person's ability to judge and recognize what is good or suitable, especially relating to such matters as art, style, beauty, and behavior." Accordingly, the

45

taste is like a skill: it is being developed throughout the entire life of an individual and may be influenced by many factors, including a person's social and cultural background, surrounding, occupation, etc. Taste is an ability to create an individual style, while fashion is a factor transforming the personal into the general.

Evaluating the situation from such a perspective, it seems that following fashion tendencies is not necessary. Though Kant believed that fashion is vanity and absurdity, he said that it is better "to be a fool in fashion than out of fashion"(Wolfendale, Kennett, 2011), as the latter option would make the people eccentrically looking old-timers. Additionally, Kant said that having a taste is important, as it establishes a basis for personal aesthetic feelings and judgments of the beautiful. With the help of taste, people discover what causes feelings of displeasure and gives joy when thinking about some object (2011). In this way, it is critically important to have a taste and develop it, especially when following some fashion tendencies.

Summing it all up, it is necessary to indicate that fashion has nothing in common with taste, as fashion is dictated by other people, while taste is developed independently. Besides, fashion is a style relevant for a particular period, while taste is an ability which is being developed throughout life. Fashion together with exquisite taste represents a perfect combination for satisfying individual aesthetic needs and creates a perfect style.

References

Cambridge Dictionary. (2017). Taste. In *The Cambridge English Dictionary*.

Dictionary.cambridge.org. Retrieved from

http://dictionary.cambridge.org/dictionary/english/taste

Wolfendale, J. & Kennett, J. (2011). *Fashion – Philosophy for Everyone: Thinking with Style* (1st ed.). Chichester, West Sussex, UK: Wiley-Blackwell.

Chapter 4. Definition Essay Writing Guide

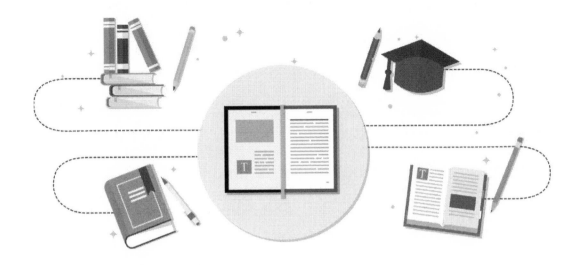

I can easily imagine your surprise or confusion after seeing the title "Definition Essay" on the content page of this book. It is not a secret that every student knows what a definition is and what are the main causes of its application. At the same time, I can predict your curiosity about this part of our guide: several sentences are enough to explain the meaning, so what is the need in writing the whole paper? Hopefully this guide will be helpful for you and clarify all issues.

What's So Special About a Definition Essay?

Answering the question raised in the introduction, it should be stated that sometimes a definition is just a small part of the essay — however, at times, the whole paper is devoted to the definition of the term. Within the definition essay, your task is "to explain the meaning of a certain term by giving a detailed description of it, and support your definition with clear examples or facts" (Writing a Definition Essay, 2012). Usually, such papers are written if the reader needs an explanation of a term, which is specific, abstract, polysemantic, or is not frequently asked.

In the academic contexts, when you are asked to write a definition paper, the essay is rather a detailed explanation given as the personal interpretation of a concrete term. Not to sound unfounded, I want to give an example for your better understanding. Two people can understand the meaning of happiness in quite different ways: you can say that happiness is to spend a day with the family, while your friend will say that happiness is to have a good sleep on the weekends. This example also suggests that it is better to choose an abstract term for a definition essay, but we will discuss it more closely in the following sections.

What else should be mentioned when talking about the specifics of a definition essay? Here are two main points that need to be addressed. First of all, please, remember that the main purpose of a definition essay is to provide a new way of looking at a particular term. By "new" in this context, I mean other than the one provided in the traditional dictionary. Of course, it does not mean that you should forget about the dictionary at all — on the contrary, any essay needs some credible source — however, the personally-written paper suggests a compilation and extension of common material with your own vision. The second point may be a paraphrase of the definition essay explanation. Such interpretation is the traditional conceptualization of the term extended by the examples. The latter is aimed at helping readers to understand the meaning of a concept or term better.

Definition Essay Writing Structure

The basic structure can be described in four parts (Definition Essay, n.d.):

1. Introduction of the defined term to the readers.

2. Presentation of clear and basic information.

3. Usage of facts, examples, or other testimony that readers will understand.

4. The mandatory final part.

What are the specifics? The definition essay, as with any other kind of essay, requires a clear thesis statement, which usually includes the term and brief definition.

Now, the presented structure needs to be discussed in more detail, just to facilitate your writing of A-grade work. I think you remember that the first part of the paper is the presentation of the topic of the essay in the format of a brief definition of the concept. Let me paraphrase — firstly, you need to define the term, and here you have several options to choose from, considering the term itself or your desire (Definition Essay, n.d.).

- You can start with the function of the defined object, which means explaining the way something works or functions.

- The other possibility is conceptualization based on the structure of the topic. In this case, you tell the readers how something is organized or should be put together.

- "Define by analysis" is one more option you can use to provide the core of your paper. I think that the name of this approach speaks for itself: you give a definition by analyzing the term in comparison with the others (usually with members of the same class). In case I have confused you with this method of presenting the core information, the following example will shed some light: *Using the method of definition by analysis, I propose you to give the definition of certain breeds of dogs by addressing the special characteristics which distinguish them from other species.*

- The last option (that we will provide in this guide) is to use the method of reverse. To say it in simple words, the author states the frames of the term by saying what it does not mean.

Of course, choosing the term or concept and defining it for the reader with a few explanatory examples is not enough to say: "I have an excellent essay, or at least I have an essay." Writing an introduction that will grab the audience's attention is important as well. My advice is to use some testimonial hook that will interest the readers. However, it is important to understand that examples, facts, or funny stories are good assistants throughout the whole paper, and therefore should not be ignored. This does not mean that it is worth filling the essay with stories and other pieces of evidence. Just select information that is the best for an explanation of the definition and that fully meets your desirable meaning. While making a choice, ask yourself: "What examples would appeal to my readers the most? Does this concrete story reveal the meaning of the term or concept? Will this particular example be the best to help an audience understand the term?" (Definition Essay, n.d.). Of course, this is not a full list of questions that will help you to write the highest quality essay, but certainly, this set will be helpful to check yourself. The rest of the questions for the personal examination will be discussed in the final section of this guide - Definition Essay Writing Checklist.

Now, as you can see, we have arrived at the stages of writing an essay, which will be discussed in detail in the following paragraphs.

Stages of Writing a Definition Essay

Before counting the steps required to complete the task of writing a definition essay successfully, I want to mention a few words. From my point of view, definition essay writing is an easier task compared to the other types discussed in this book. But do not relax, because good preparation and understanding of what needs to be done is the first step to an excellent essay. That is why my recommendation will be to follow each of the steps carefully, but at the same time, do not forget about imagination and using your own ideas:

1. Choose a term you want to explain and introduce it to the readers. In fact, this stage can be divided into two substages: choice and presentation. The first may seem to be easy, but try to limit your term before actually defining it. For example, the term "family" may be narrowed to the explanation of the terms "nuclear family" and "extended family." Considering the second substage, previously we mentioned several ways to cope with this task. Just keep in your memory that the main task of this stage is to indicate the context and future content of the paper clearly.

2. The next step is deep research with the use of several sources, such as encyclopedias, dictionaries, and studies. The goal of such study is an understanding of the common definition of the term. On the one hand, you can use these combinations to give the primary definition on your own. On the other hand, some controversial aspects or the ones requiring clarification will be observed. Anyway, the analysis of data gathered during this step will allow you to create a unique definition of the chosen term or concept.

3. Now you are ready to present the term to your readers. This means that the next step is creating the introductory part of the essay.

4. After the introduction, the time comes for the main body paragraphs. This part of the paper serves as the presentation of information about the term to the readers. The body of the definition essay is devoted to the personal interpretation of the term or concept, and cases when they are used. Also, some information about the origins and historical development together with the evolution of the use can be included in the writing. A little advice about the main part of the definition essay will be to highlight, if possible, mistakes often committed by ordinary usage of the term.

5. Think about examples and include them as an illustration and explanation of the definition. Some tips about choice were already discussed in the previous section of the guide.

6. Finally, summarize your main ideas in a succinct conclusion.

Now, knowing the structure of the definition essay and the major steps of its writing, you are ready for mastering your paper with helpful tips and suggestions.

Guidelines and Tightening Your Essay

Every day, people are faced with many terms and concepts but do not even think about them. Surely there is some sort of a social contract concerning the meaning of the majority of concepts, and we know them as the common interpretation of the subjects. At the same time, there are plenty of terms, usually abstract or scientific, that collect the "discussions" around their meanings and definitions. Not to be unfounded, we agree that everybody knows what a table or computer is, but it is hard to find a global consensus about the meaning of love or beauty, or heroism. Based on this, a list of good topic examples was compiled and will be presented below.

Good Topic Examples

1. What makes someone a hero?

2. What is success?

3. Explain the definition of beauty.

4. What is happiness?

5. How can one define respect?

6. What is the definition of loyalty?

7. What is friendship?

8. What is your definition of intelligence?

9. Explain morale in your own words.

10. How can you explain masculinity and femininity?

11. What do you mean by the concept of privacy?

12. How can one define fashion?

13. A good wife or husband: who are they?

14. Present your explanation of the American dream.

15. How can you define success?

Useful Tips for Writing a Definition Essay

1. Advice of top importance is to understand that providing the definition is not copying and pasting the information from credible (or even worse, from unreliable) sources. At the same time, no one wants you to create the new definition for the well-known terms or established concepts. Therefore, writing a definition essay means to introduce the readers to your interpretation of the term based on the already existing meanings.

2. In order to avoid confusing your readers with the wrong definition and interpretation, the chosen term should be understood by you personally as well. Only, in this case, you will be able to apply some personal experience to the explanation. At the same time, there is no prohibition to use the task to write an essay with the aim to understand a new topic or to learn something new. Just be sure to comprehend the material completely and adequately present it to the general public.

3. It was already mentioned above but should be repeated one more time: there are several approaches to the definition of any term or concept by explaining its functions, structure, or nature,

by specifying what it does not mean, or by comparing it with other members of the same class of words and emphasizing the differences (How to Write a Definition Essay, 2015). The choice is yours.

4. Another point that was already discussed but needs repeating is the need to follow a structure. Remember that the presentation of the term is given in the introduction, the extended explanations and examples are presented in the main body, while the essay is concluded with brief summarizing sentences.

5. Another tip is to avoid the use of "when," "where," and other similar words while formulating the definition.

6. The final advice is to adhere to the tradition of defining the noun with the use of a noun, adjective with an adjective, and so on following a similar logic.

If you have reached this part of the guide, you are already able to write a perfect definition essay. I want to assure you that there is no doubt in your abilities; however, I still want to make sure that this book gives you as much useful practical information as possible. That is why it is worth paying attention to the fundamental mistakes that are made by students in writing essays of the definition type.

Mistakes to Avoid While Writing a Definition Essay

I think you have noticed that each guide has the same structure, but still the kind of presentation varies depending on the features of the essay types. If you did not notice it before, now you know for sure that this is true. Indeed, if all possible and common errors were just listed with bullet points, you would lose interest.

Regarding this, I hope that you, dear readers, love to make lists as much as I do. For the definition essay, I have decided to present the mistakes that need to be avoided while writing definition essays by analogy with the popular "to do list" format. Below you can find the table Do and Do Not, which will help you to deal with this section.

Do	Do Not
Narrow the term to ease the process of creating the definition type of essay. For example, it will take a lot of time and pages to explain the term "love," but you can choose "platonic" as the topic of your essay and save time and energy.	It is not worth it to narrow the topic excessively or to write about a well-known and obvious term.
As in any other type of essay, use transitions and linking words to connect the parts of the paper to make it look like solid text, rather than individual pieces taken from the dictionary.	Even though your task is to give a detailed explanation to your audience about your vision of the term or concept, there is no need for an overly detailed manner of presentation. The readers will quickly get tired and may not even finish reading the whole paper.
Try to provide a unique definition. Remember that no one sees the world as you do, therefore, no one can explain the concrete term or concept as you can. Creativity and aspiration to find a non-standard explanation is a good strategy.	Do not repeat "the defined term within the bounds of the definition itself" (Writing a Definition Essay, 2012). This means that the term "panic fear" does not become more understandable for people if you write "it is a fear that…"
Proofreading the final version of the text is the key to success and a definition essay that deserves the highest mark.	It was already mentioned, but do not use structures like "A is when" or "B is where" while creating the definition. A good example is paraphrasing the definition "Totalitarianism is when the state tries to control the society" into "Totalitarianism is a political

	regime which presumes that the state holds authority over society…" (Writing a Definition Essay, 2012).

If this Do and Do Not format is not to your liking, here is a list of the most widespread mistakes students make while coping with writing definition essays:

- They forget to highlight the term that they are defining throughout the entire paper. This is an unforgivable mistake because there is a high chance that someone will not understand what the essay is about.

- They try to define a term that has a common interpretation and about which there is no debate.

- They think that a detailed and clear definition is enough for the readers' understanding. Therefore, students often do not cite any examples and illustrations, which, in turn, only confuses the readers and makes it difficult for them to understand conditions of the term's usage.

- And finally: they copy the definition word-for-word or with little to no paraphrasing. Students are often afraid of going beyond the boundaries and creating something innovative.

Definition Essay Writing Checklist

- Has the term you've chosen been narrowed enough, and does it not have a generally accepted meaning?

- Have you provided readers with a clear definition of the term or concept? Does the definition contain a concept which is explained? Did you omit using "when," "where," and similar words while creating your definition?

- Is your research deep enough to present credible information to your readers?

- Is the definition explained enough to be understood by a person who has no idea about the particular word and its meaning?

- Is the balance between informational content and interest in the topic sustained in your essay? Will it be interesting and appealing to the reader?

- Did you use examples, quotes, stories, and other types of testimony? Were they illustrative for an ordinary audience?

- Did you provide credible sources of the definition together with more personalized pieces of evidence and interpretations?

- Did you check the grammar, punctuation, and logic of presenting the ideas in your definition essay?

References

Definition Essay. (2015). In *Essay Info Writing Guides*. Retrieved from

http://essayinfo.com/essays/definition_essay.php

How to Write a Definition Essay. (2016). In *EssayPro*. Retrieved from

https://essaypro.com/blog/definition-essay/

Writing a Definition Essay. (2012). In *Academic Help*. Retrieved from

https://academichelp.net/academic-assignments/essay/write-definition-essay.html

Sample 1. Defining Charisma

Charisma is a mysterious concept. It has existed for about 2000 years and originally meant "divine flavor." Now one of the interpretations of the word "charisma" is the ability to influence others. It is easier to understand what charisma is than to give a definition to it. In various newspapers, magazines and articles, there are examples of charismatic leaders: John F. Kennedy, Martin Luther King, Barack Obama. However, the description of charisma as such can be hardly found there. As the notion is of particular interest, this paper focuses on the investigation of the word "charisma" in the historical context.

The concept of charisma goes back to the Apostle Paul's appeal around 50 AD. There is a first written mention of the word "charisma," which was derived from the Greek word "charis," meaning "gift," "flavor." Paul defines charisma as a "divine flavor" or as a "gift of God."

Paul considered charisma as a mystical concept. People believed that the divine gifts might influence any person without the mediation of religious institutions. There was no such concept as leadership charisma. Complementary gifts of flavor aimed to serve communities without the help of an imposed leader. However, in approximately the 4th century under the active influence of the church, the concept of "charisma" had not already meant anything derived directly from the Holy Spirit. The church wanted it to be understood in the context of the church hierarchy, on top of which bishops were located. They interpreted divine laws described in the Bible in their own way. The former concept of charisma survived only because of heretics. There were preachers among them who advocated the idea of getting divine inspiration directly without the appeal to the bishops or the Holy Scriptures. The church violently persecuted this kind of "heresy."

The concept of charisma has not been mentioned for several centuries. The interest in it appeared again only in the 20th century when German sociologist Max Weber appealed to it in his works. In fact, we owe the modern meaning of "charisma" to him. He interpreted Apostle Paul's religious ideas in the context of sociological concepts of power and leadership. Weber defined charisma as the quality of an extraordinary individual, thanks to which they are assessed as endowed with supernatural, superhuman or at least specifically exceptional powers and properties unavailable to others. His ideas were used in politics and culture. The first "charismatic" political leaders were Benito Mussolini and Adolf Hitler. Therefore, many European thinkers concluded that the manifestations of charismatic authority entailed sinister events.

The first charismatic politicians famous for not manipulative, but positive features were John F. Kennedy and his brother Robert Kennedy. After 60 years of the 20th century, the word "charisma" became actively used. It was also applied not only to political leaders but to prominent personalities, famous in other fields, such as Mohammed Ali.

Currently, the concept of "charisma" is used to describe certain personalities, politicians, celebrities and businessmen. Under this concept, we understand a special inherent quality that distinguishes people from the masses and attracts them to other people.

Charisma is a quality related to a special talent. For example, American politicians who possess qualities of a charismatic leader are Bill Clinton and Barack Obama. They are currently the only two to have such an honorary title.

In the business world, an example of a charismatic leader is undoubtedly Steve Jobs. Farsighted and inspiring and at the same time changeable and unstable in his mood. Among the celebrities, while most of the entertainment industry is devoted to the fabrication of "stars" of the show "Idols" and "The Voice," charisma is a sign of a rare and genuine talent. This is what a reality show can not create.

References

The Enchanting History of Charisma. (2016). *History Extra*. Retrieved from

http://www.historyextra.com/article/premium/enchanting-history-charisma

Eatwell, R., 2006. The Concept and Theory of Charismatic Leadership. *Totalitarian Movements and Political Religions*, 7 (2), pp. 141-156.

Derman, J. (2011). Max Weber and Charisma: A Transatlantic Affair. *New German Critique*, 38, 51, 88.

Sample 2. What Makes Someone a Hero?

To begin with, it has to be said that all of us know there are a variety of life situations that sometimes require us to be heroic. Somebody calls for help, and you try to help this person. Or someone is drowning, and you deliberate whether to help or not because you are afraid to die or because you cannot swim. I suppose everyone has heard these stories, but indeed a very few people have witnessed them. Therefore, a dilemma occurs. How to define the term "hero" when only a few people have this experience while others have never witnessed it? That's why this question has to be discussed and analyzed further in the essay.

First of all, it must be pointed out that a look at the reasons why people act heroically has to to be taken. In fact, the question is: what is the main motive of acting immediately while others are standing, and watching? The article "What Makes a Hero?" claims that the two factors that have a great impact on people's decision about acting heroically are "the circumstances they find themselves in and how they react to these circumstances (i.e. the characteristics of the person involved)."

These are the factors that influence the decision people make during the first seconds of the situation happening. Therefore, as it can be noticed, the questions are: what are the circumstances that lead to this kind of situation and what is our reaction to the problem?

Secondly, it has to be highlighted that Philip Zimbardo, author of "What Makes a Hero?" tries to answer the question: why do people act brave and heroic? Why are some people good while others act badly and cowardly? Zimbardo comes to a conclusion that the crucial answer to the question "What makes us evil?" can be found. However, when we ask people why they become heroic, no precise answer can be found. Thus, as it can be seen, there can be a great variety of reasons why people act heroically, but there is no actual research that can prove these assumptions.

In addition, it must be mentioned that the term "hero" is quite dual. On the one hand, you are not afraid of taking risks no matter what the outcome will be, but on the other hand, you are ready to help other people that need your help in that particular moment. Thus, it has to be underlined that Philip Zimbardo tells the readers that "the key to heroism is a concern for other people in need — a concern to defend a moral cause, knowing there is a personal risk, done without expectation of reward" (2011). And, in my opinion, it is the best definition of the term "heroism." This definition serves to explain the term the best.

Finally, it has to be said that all of us know there is a great number of life situations that sometimes require us to be heroic. As a matter of fact, there can be many reasons why people act heroically, but there is no actual research that can prove these assumptions. Therefore, the main questions to ask are: what are the circumstances that lead to this kind of situation and what is our reaction to the problem? As a result, it has to be highlighted that heroism means acting due to your own moral principles knowing about the personal risk. Thus, to my mind, it is the best definition of the term "hero" nowadays.

References

What Makes a Hero? *History's Heroes?* (n.d.). Retrieved from

    http://historysheroes.e2bn.org/whatisahero/whatmakesahero

Zimbardo, P. (2011). What Makes a Hero? *History's Heroes?* Retrieved from

    http://greatergood.berkeley.edu/article/item/what_makes_a_hero

Chapter 5. Descriptive Essay Writing Guide

It can be assumed that there is not a single person who has not heard the phrase "a picture is worth a thousand words." These words may be taken on faith; however, there is a question that remains open: "How can we find a thousand words to describe the picture?" This question is asked by all students who received the task to write a descriptive essay and want to complete it successfully.

First of all, let us remember those recognized as masters of the pen: authors like Shakespeare, Charles Dickens, and Jane Austin. While reading their text, you don't simply become a participant of the described events, but have a feeling that you have been transported to the surroundings of the events. How did they achieve such an effect? The answer is, of course, with the help of the descriptions. Do not be afraid, because nobody is expecting you to become a new Shakespeare, but you can at least master your skills of creating descriptive essays and try.

What's So Special About a Descriptive Essay?

Generally speaking, the explanation of the term "descriptive essay" comes up from the title — it is a genre of writing in which the author gives a depiction of something — it can be an object, a person, situation, or experience. No matter what you have or want to describe, the painted image should be vivid to be able to move in the mind of the audience — in other words, to make them feel your emotions, live your experience, or imagine your best friend.

A descriptive essay is the most creative type of paper that any student may face during his or her academic path. It is not surprising because a descriptive writing product requires not only being informative, but also picturesque, transmitting images through language and vocabulary. Some experts believe that the descriptive essay is the only genre in the academic sphere that "encourages the student's ability to create a written account of a particular experience. What is more, this genre allows for a great deal of artistic freedom" (Baker, Brizee, & Angeli, 2013). Based on this information, it can be concluded that the main goal of a descriptive essay is "to create a vivid experience for the reader" (Baker, Brizee, & Angeli, 2013).

Starting from the goal, we can say that there are several strategies for achieving the purpose. Let us remember that any information a person faces is interpreted only after its perception via one of the senses. It was proved that the most efficient representation of something could be achieved through taste, touch, smell, hearing, or sight (Tips on Writing a Descriptive Essay, n.d.); therefore, if you want to succeed while creating a descriptive piece of writing, the best strategy will be to appeal to one or all of the senses.

Another point that should be noticed, when talking about the specifics of the descriptive essay, is the possibility of dividing several subtypes. In fact, the main criterion for subtypes is the characteristic of the subject that is the basis of the description. If you feel a little confusion about this idea, I can assure you — there is no need to worry. In simple words, while choosing the topic of a future descriptive essay, you may decide whether you want to depict a person, place, memory, experience, or object. Respectively, for each of the categories, there is a subtype for the descriptive essay.

There is one more important note before we move on to the structure and stages of creating the descriptive essay. Whatever topic you have chosen, and no matter what subtype of the descriptive essay you have decided to produce, the essay should contain the purpose. It should be highlighted that descriptive essays are not written just to describe something or somebody, but the author should make the paper significant. The goal may be to understand the lesson from the experience or the story of the object's impact on your life (How to Write a Descriptive Essay, 2015). Just make sure that your work is not meaningless.

Descriptive Essay Writing Structure

The first advice concerning the structure is to create a structured (excuse me for tautology) outline before you actually start writing the paper. In fact, this idea is related to any type of essay discussed within this book; however, I have decided to place it in this guide, because, in the case of the descriptive essay, an outline is a tool for organizing thought, as well as an assistant for making the essay flow better.

Returning to the subject of this guide's section, the structure of any descriptive essay reflects the traditional structure of academic texts: there is an introduction, a body, and a conclusion.

Introduction

- Start the introduction with a hook sentence. It is even not worth mentioning that it is the introduction which draws the readers' attention. Similarly, it becomes clear that the most important part in this case, is the first sentence, also known as "the hook." Of course, the author should try to make the entire essay full of vivid descriptions — however, the primary purpose at this stage is to grab the attention from the very beginning.

- The next part is a presentation of the subject that you are writing about. However, it should be more subdued, so that you will not disclose all the cards at once.

- An author can include brief background information. This means that you can add some interesting details about the subject of the essay. However, try to adopt more restrained language (of course, if you do not want to lose the attention before the real description starts).

- Finally, the introduction should contain the appeal to the five senses (they were mentioned in the previous section of the guide, in case you have already forgotten or decided to read the guide from this part). The author, of course, has a choice to select one or some combination, or even, if you are creative enough, to use all of them.

Body paragraph or paragraphs

Please note that the number of the paragraphs and therefore the length of the essay depends on the length of the story or information about the subject. Also, you should take into account the formal requirements of the teacher and objectively assess your own writing skills.

To avoid losing the reader's attention (of course, if you were able to grab it in the first place), the body of the essay should be started from an exciting point. No one wants to read the boring prehistory or the description, so give some really exciting pictures, and then you can return to some previous explanations, in order not to lose the thread of the story or description.

Another critical point concerning the body paragraph or paragraphs is to continue appealing to the senses. Some people say, "anyone can tell a story, but not everybody can do it well" (How to Write a Descriptive Essay, 2015), so you should do your best, and this is one of the options.

Do not forget to include factual material and details. It may sound like one of the tips in a series about how to avoid gaps or increasing the number of words, but the tips will actually be discussed in the further sections. The facts and details help your reader to think about and be interested in the described issues.

While planning and creating the outline of the descriptive essay, remember this proven fact: "people's attention starts at a high point, gradually decreases, but comes back sky-high with the finale" (How to Write a Descriptive Essay, 2015). Be sure that the finale was worth the time spent on reading the rest of the essay.

Conclusion

Quench the curiosity of the readers in the reflection. State the purpose of the story or description (the significance of the goal was discussed in the specifics of the descriptive essay). Reading descriptive, bright and vivid language is a useful and interesting pastime, but the audience will be even more interested to know what determined your decision to describe this issue, or thing, or person.

A good author can predict what moment will be the most interesting or, on the other hand, the least clear. In any case, these points need some additional explanation, especially the ones about significance.

Use a clincher statement. A good descriptive essay does not lose the attention of readers after they finish reading. The hook in the final sentence may solve this problem — for example, the rhetorical question stimulates people to return with their thoughts to your essay. Therefore, essays are better to end with a clincher in the form of an intriguing thought, quotation, or question (How to Write a Descriptive Essay, 2015).

Stages of Writing a Descriptive Essay

The previous part of this guide was devoted to the structure of a paper written in the descriptive style, but the presentation of the material began with specifying what is necessary to make an outline for a future productive and successful work. Within this section, the issue of the writing process will be observed in more detail and presented as a four-stage plan.

1. Choose the topic and create the outline.

As it can be understood, the creation of the outline may be included in this step; however, you should not forget about one more issue that is no less important, and actually, should be done before the outline preparation — the topic choice. In this type of essay, the topic should not present something unusual or popular. Rather you should show your skills to turn an ordinary subject into something really interesting and worthwhile.

First of all, determine the subtype of the descriptive essay — whether it will be the closest person or the most awkward moment in your life. Just try to understand why you want to describe this subject. Then you can start the outline by defining the qualities that will be described and feelings that will be associated. After planning each paragraph separately, focus on the logical transitions between them and the appropriate sequence.

2. Write the draft of the descriptive essay.

At this stage you should follow the outline of the essay — however, it is important to create an essay which is worthy of being read. Remember to add poetic language and words connected to the senses. "Write, so the reader will see the sunset, hear the song, smell the flowers, taste the pie, or feel the touch of a hand" (Tips on Writing a Descriptive Essay, n.d.). Just keep in mind the goal to give the audience some sort of experience they do not have.

3. Revise the prepared paper.

The name of this phase speaks for itself. You test the entire essay on yourself — just imagine that you are the reader and think what parts sounds good, where there is a need for modifications, and whether some explanations and descriptions are useful or useless.

4. Edit the text.

After the text was reviewed and necessary corrections were made, the proofreading phase of the text takes place. An author should be accurate in checking the grammar and structure of sentences, while not forgetting about the appropriate descriptive style of language. It is usually recommended another person to read and evaluate the essay from another side and give an objective assessment.

After completing all four stages, you can safely publish the descriptive essay and present it to classmates and the professor.

Guidelines and Tightening Your Essay

Of course, the choice of the topic is the most important and, at the same time, the most challenging task while writing a descriptive essay. In this section, possible issues considering the subtypes are presented to help you define the topic for your future papers.

Good Topic Examples

Person

1. Define traits that make the person a good role model.

2. Describe the strangest person in your community.

3. What makes your friend stand out compared to the rest of your acquaintances?

Place

4. Describe your secret place.

5. What would be the ideal place to meet a friend?

6. Paint a picture of the fantastic world you would like to live in.

Memory

7. What event has become your favorite memory?

8. Describe the characteristics that make an ordinary event the unique memory of your life.

9. What is the memory you would like to forget?

Experience

10. Describe a moment in your life where you either led a crowd or did something completely out of your comfort zone!

11. What do you think is an experience that everybody should go through?

12. Describe the most challenging situation in your life and how you dealt with it.

Object

13. Imagine that you will meet an alien, and think about the way you will describe our planet.

14. Describe something that you would bury in a time capsule to tell people in the future about what life is like today.

15. Describe objects that you will take to a desert island.

Useful Tips for Descriptive Essay Writing

It may seem that this guide is full of tips on how to write a successful essay without extra effort. So, it is quite logical that the question about the importance of this section arises. Personally, I hold the opinion that there are no extra suggestions, so here are some more guidelines to edit your essay.

1. **Allocate time for brainstorming**. It is useful to record all ideas, so you can evaluate them and discard the unnecessary and unsuccessful.

2. **Use clear language**. Of course, a description essay requires the use of beautiful and emotional vocabulary, but remember that your readers should understand your points — therefore, consider the relevance to the subject and audience.

3. **Do not forget about the senses**. As it was already mentioned, they help to establish a connection with the reader.

4. **Leave the reader with a clear understanding** of what you were trying to say.

5. **Be organized while planning your essay**. Everything should look logical, and not just for you but for the entire audience of the descriptive essay.

6. **Compare the process of writing a descriptive essay with a painting** created by an artist. Your task is to give all-inclusive impressions to your readers.

Mistakes to Avoid While Writing a Descriptive Essay

Usually, a list of mistakes (even the most common mistakes) looks like a shopping list for the whole week. In this guide, I have decided to concentrate on three main errors related to writing in descriptive style.

Using long strings of adjectives. There is no doubt that adjectives play an important part of descriptive essays. Moreover, it can be said that adjectives are the core of the composition in the descriptive style. Regarding this fact, it is not surprising that students abuse their use in descriptive papers. The advice is to limit the number to three adjectives consecutively, as using too many of them is a sign that the student has exhausted his or her thoughts and only uses a thesaurus to increase the length of the text, and it sounds more pretentious.

Quite a common mistake is refusing to use metaphors and similarities. Being passionate with the adjectives, writers often forget about other linguistic tools, which can be even more poetic and, without a doubt, have greater appeal to the senses. This is about metaphors, which are widely used by professional authors, and comparisons, which help to understand even completely unfamiliar things. For example, instead of writing, "His eyes were blue," the author can say, "His eyes were seas," or "His eyes were as blue as the deep sea." This example illustrates how a metaphor in the first case and simile in the second fill the words with emotional and descriptive power.

Finally, students often forget to organize the essay properly. In fact, students often do not attach much importance to the structure of a descriptive essay (at least not as much as in the case of argumentative or cause and effect essays). Well, the nature of the descriptive style really dictates a lower degree of dependence on a rigid structure; however, you should not ignore the logic of the narration. You cannot leave the descriptive essay to chance, as any idea must be in a proper place and serve a common idea — to absorb the attention of readers. And do not forget to use transitions that will guide the audience through the paper.

Descriptive Essay Writing Checklist

- Does the essay contain enough description of the situation, object, memory, person, or place?

- Are there any paragraphs that confuse readers more than they describe the subject of the essay?

- Do both the word choice and figurative language involve appealing to the five senses? Does the vocabulary transmit emotions and meaning?

- Were there enough details included so that the reader can see a complete picture?

- Did you clearly state the purpose of writing the descriptive essay? Consider whether this purpose is clear to the reader.

- Does your "hook" communicate balance between the interest and the discovery of the essence of the whole description?

- Was the conclusion quite unambiguous, and did it contained some instrument to keep the public's attention after they read the text?

At the end, ask yourself once again why you decided to write about this experience, memory, person, object or place. Make sure that you have included such aspirations in your text. After checking the final version of the essay, you are surely ready for independent and creative work, so look for the inspiration and write descriptive essays!

References

Baker, J., Brizee, A., Angeli, E. (2013). Descriptive Essays. In *Purdue Online Writing Lab*. Retrieved from https://owl.english.purdue.edu/owl/resource/685/03/

Descriptive Essay. (n.d.). How Do You Write a Descriptive Essay: Avoiding Common Mistakes. In *Motive Art*. Retrieved from http://www.motive-art.org/what-mistakes-you-should-avoid-in-your-descriptive-essay

How to Write a Descriptive Essay. (2015). In *EssayPro*. Retrieved from https://essaypro.com/blog/definition-essay/

Tips on Writing a Descriptive Essay. (n.d.). In *Time 4 Writing*. Retrieved from http://www.time4writing.com/writing-resources/descriptive-essay/

Sample 1. Describe a Smartphone to a Time Traveler from the 1900s

In the twenty-first century, almost everyone has a small flat colorful device. People wear them in pockets and bags, then take them out and look at them smiling, surprised, or irritated, talk to them asking questions, telling stories, or shouting, touch them, shake them or even beat them sometimes. These are not the pets, bred in the 2000s—these are smartphones. With more than one billion users around the world, they can be called a symbol of the third millennium (Reisinger, 2012).

I have described them as a tiny device, but the modern smartphones are similar to a sheet of paper more. They are extremely thin, and, similarly to paper, they also can contain text and images. And yet, the smartphones weight more — you can feel that pleasant heaviness in your hand. They are made from metal, which forms their back surface, and glass, which makes up the front. It looks like a black mirror when the phone is not active, but as you touch the cool surface of glass, the screen suddenly lights up with thousands of colors. With the same unexpectedness, the smartphone can ring. No need to panic, there is no orchestra hidden in the next room or around the corner. It is just a smartphone.

As a time traveler from the 1900s, you probably know what a telephone is. The smartphone can be called its offspring, or, more precisely, its grandchild. The major function of the smartphone remained the same — it enables people to talk with each other over a distance. Nevertheless, its design has noticeably changed, as well as its tasks.

The father of the smartphone and the son of the telephone was the cell phone. It can also be called a mobile phone because it had no wires and can be easily transported. The first cell phone call took place on April 3, 1973. At the press conference at Hilton hotel in Manhattan, Martin Cooper, the general manager of the system division of Motorola, demonstrated the first prototype of the wireless phone. This model of the phone, DynaTAC, resembled a boot — it was thin and long, had a protruding "lip," and also an antenna. He made a few calls, and the phone functioned flawlessly. The conference was a success and became a starting point in the history of cellphones

(Woyke, 2014). On the contrary, the smartphone does not have a precise birthday. The most common version dates the smartphone back to 2007, when Steve Jobs introduced the first iPhone. Nevertheless, experts point out that many of the smartphone's features were already available on other devices, such as personal digital assistants, and messaging devices such as the early Blackberry phones.

But what is the difference between the cell phone and the smartphone? Unlike the former, the smartphone has an open operational system. It means that the user can download new applications designed by other developers, which will extend the functions of the phone. You probably have several questions now. For example, "what is the application?" It is a program which can have different functions. If you look at the smartphone screen, you can see big white numbers. As you can guess, it is a clock. Or, when I touch this little square on the screen that looks like a camera — this is actually a camera, like those bulky machines you used to take photographs in the 1900s, just smaller. You can notice it on the other side of the phone — it looks like a tiny glass bird eye. These applications, the clock and the camera, are already installed on the smartphone when it is produced. Nevertheless, it is also possible to buy the new ones in a store. They can be downloaded from the Internet — a global network, which connects computers, tablets, and smartphones.

As you see, the smartphone is both a very good-looking and practical invention. It allows the user to talk, to take photos, to read books, and to do thousands of other things. It is a technological breakthrough of the twenty-first century that helps to make billions of lives worldwide more comfortable and exciting. If you manage to take one of them back with you, to the 1900s, it will undoubtedly surprise your contemporaries.

References

Reisinger, D. (2012). Worldwide Smartphone User Base Hits 1 Billion. *CNET*. Retrieved from

https://www.cnet.com/news/worldwide-smartphone-user-base-hits-1-billion/

Woyke, E. (2014). *The Smartphone: Anatomy of an Industry* (1st ed.). New York: The New Press.

Sample 2. My Favorite Bookstore

The bookstore "Bookish Style" is one of the great places to catch the latest bestseller. It is necessary to understand that the bookstore is not only about purchasing something to read, but about atmosphere and a good collection. That is why the sensory observation is quite significant to consider when entering such a store, because each bookstore has its own atmosphere which inspires, makes the reader feel better, and encourages the creation of new ideas.

To begin with, according to my childhood memories when I first entered the bookstore, it made me feel excited, as this place implies boosting of all five senses, including sight, hearing, smell, taste and touch. For instance, the ability to look at an object and memorize what it looked like with just a moment of observation is a good illustration of sensory memory, which separated these feelings from all the others.

When a person comes to the bookstore, at first sight, it gives a unique and special perception. There are enormous windows which provide a majestic and exceptional look, while also giving more light to the store so that there is more desire appearing for me to choose a book observing the whole store.

Furthermore, the smell of "Bookish Style" cannot be compared to anything else. Just after walking inside it, one can feel the flow of ideas and the strong smell of paper coming from the books surrounding you and wishing to be picked up and read. There is always an old smell of the sheets of many books or even magazines, and the ones which are resting on the shelves. Even the smell of dust covering some of them makes me feel different.

To my mind, touching the covers of the antique and new books gives me a whole new outlook concerning them. The feeling which appears when holding one and turning papers is entirely different from holding an e-Book, though the market has become full of them for the last decades. Due to their weight, it is even easier to make a choice as it means that various advantages and disadvantages should be considered. For instance, whether I need it for the trip and do not want

73

it to be heavy when carrying it around or if the purpose is strictly educational so that the more it has information, the better.

In addition, one more vital factor of my frequent visiting of this very bookstore is the sounds (Collins, 2006). I can hear nothing but the calm and somehow friendly noises of pages turning. As it is the best place for my imaginary skills to start working, it becomes even possible to hear other minds thinking. The temperature of the store air conditioner, in its turn, makes it so pleasant to read a book and stay there longer. There are always people with completely different aims but all inspired to learn something new, educate themselves, and they are people with the same interests as mine.

It is important to take the taste into consideration as well (Collins, 2006). When coming to the "Bookish Style" bookstore, the desire to sit comfortably in a quiet place with a cup of herbal tea and a little bowl of biscuits emerges immediately. That is why there is a cafeteria inside which is a great marketing move, I must admit.

To conclude, all bookstores are special and they have the power to evoke all the sensory experiences at the same time. Moreover, they improve memory, imagination and generate ideas in minds about what is important for self-development. Therefore, I would recommend everyone to read real books instead of using innovational devices.

References

Brynie, F. (2009). *Brain Sense* (1st ed.). New York: American Management Association.

Collins, A. (2006). *See, Hear, Smell, Taste, and Touch* (1st ed.). Washingtion, DC: NationalGeographic.

Gregory, C. (2008). "But I Want a Real Book": An Investigation of Undergraduates' Usage and Attitudes Toward Electronic Books. *Reference & User Services Quarterly*, *47*(3).

Chapter 6. Expository Essay Writing Guide

First of all, I want to assure you that we have not fallen into a parallel universe where there are other types of academic papers. Do not let this word, which looks quite scientific, fool you because you undoubtedly have already faced and written at least one expository essay (even without knowing this fact).

Frankly speaking, during the preparation of this guide I caught myself thinking that information about expository essays varies a lot and causes confusion. You can find sources that provide a long definition where expository writing is a whole category in which other types are included (such as descriptive, comparison, cause and effect). At the same time, your search can easily lead to the explanations where expository essays equate to "how to" essays. That is why within this guide, we will try to sort out what an expository essay is, what stages should be completed, and how to write it successfully.

What's So Special About an Expository Essay?

The first question that should be answered may be formulated the following way: what will help us to understand what an expository essay actually is? What about a proposition to start with the term "expository" itself? Merriam-Webster Dictionary states that this adjective is used "to describe writing that is done to explain something." Of course, it simplifies the task for us, so we can say that an expository essay is a paper written with the goal to introduce the reader to the topic: to explore it and to talk about it.

Having dealt with the first issue, we can move to the second question, which sounds just the same as the title of this guide's section. The main point here is to draw your attention to specifics (as we will call it), which, in fact, is the need to stay in the defined position while writing an expository essay. Some sources advise to keep in mind the debate style of thinking when you should defend your position and disprove the opposite (Writing an Expository Essay, 2012). However, there is no need to be extremely categorical; remember that you are not writing a persuasive or argumentative essay. The presence of a clear position rather means that you should not speak on topics that correlate (especially poorly) with the chosen issue. In other words, the author operates just the fact that supports his or her position.

To understand what expository essay writing is, we should know its components, so the next part will be devoted to the structure of any expository essay.

Expository Essay Writing Structure

Taking into account the fact that reading this fact may be the first time you see the word collocation "expository essay," you may expect to see an absolutely new and unfamiliar structure. I must disappoint you, dear readers, because once again you have to work with the standard five-paragraph structure. Nevertheless, in the information below, you can find not only a description of what you probably already know but also additional pieces of advice adjusted for an expository essay writing style.

Introduction

Opening sentence. Like any other piece of writing, an expository essay should start with a statement that serves to catch the reader's attention. This first sentence is better to address the reviewing of the topic in order to present it to the audience. If you want to bring creativity into the essay, you can choose a quotation, question, fact, definition, dilemma, or even the position opposing the one you have selected as the introductory statement.

Context. The topic, in general, may be misinterpreted by the readers, so you need to provide some additional information to set up the tone and to direct the thoughts of the readers.

Thesis statement. The thesis statement is the most important and challenging part of any essay (an expository essay is not an exception). In this short sentence, do not forget to highlight your arguable position which will be supported in the body part of the expository essay.

Body Paragraphs

Topic sentence. Each paragraph in the body must be started with the sentence that provides the main idea for the particular piece of paper (the whole paragraph in this case).

Supporting evidence. After claiming the concrete idea, it should be supported by evidence. In this case, you as an author are not limited in choice: you can use textual evidence, statistics, first-person interviews, and your own experience.

Please note! Plagiarism is a serious issue in the academic sphere, so be attentive to the references. This is especially true for the textual evidence, such as citations, paraphrasing, and the summary.

Analysis. Using examples to defend your idea is great — however, it is not enough for readers. Your task is to justify the choice of the concrete evidence and its significance as an illustration of the idea and thesis statement.

Transition. Use linking words and phrases to facilitate the process of following your idea for the audience.

Conclusion

The basic part of all papers is the summary of the whole work. Putting ideas described in the entire essay into several sentences may be no less challenging than writing a strong thesis for the paper.

Note that the conclusion is not just a list of your thoughts presented within the text. You should show your analytical abilities as well — make the final part a compilation of all the information.

Stages of Writing an Expository Essay

It goes without saying that writing the original text is hard work, and usually accompanied by anxious doubts: "Will I be able to create something interesting?" "What should be the first step?" "What should I write about?" "How should I complete the text?" The writer, naturally, would like to know the available and unambiguous answers to these burning questions. That is why more and more students today suffer from procrastination, which results in the situation of having to write all papers the night before the deadline. To avoid such cases, you should remember to begin as early as possible to create the most interesting expository essay that deserves the highest grade.

The most obvious point here is to understand that there are no definite answers for any of the mentioned questions. There are only different methods for creating essays of different types, and everyone is free to choose which path is most suitable for them. Below you can find the most common method of structuring the process of writing an expository essay.

1. Think about the audience. This step can be included in the wider planning phase that is obligatory in case you want to achieve a good final product. You need to understand the needs and expectations of your future readers, as well as their attributes that determine the interests and therefore the topic. If an expository essay is one of your assignments for university, do not forget about the professor's instructions (as he or she will be a part of your audience); include everything that is expected by your instructor (How to Write an Expository Essay, 2015).

2. Choose the topic. As it was already stated, knowing your audience means knowing topics to talk about. By this time you may decide that it is the easiest part; however, choosing a topic is quite challenging. You should balance between personal interest and the interest of your audience. You can find some useful pieces of advice related to this stage in the next section of this guide Guidelines and Tightening Your Essay.

3. Conduct research. Please note — even the best thoughts and the strongest thesis are nothing without proper evidence. Think about your topic and several arguments for or against your position, then find some testimony supporting these points. Of course, if you do not know your arguments yet, you can firstly do some research and only then formulate the main arguments. In any sequence, select sources that provide significant support in your case and do not forget about their credibility (please note that the latter also includes relevance and novelty of information).

4. Create an outline. This step will help you to say exactly what you want to say. There is no doubt that much can be said about the topic of your choice; however, in the case of an essay (especially an expository essay) it is better to get straight to the point — an outline will help you to weed out the superfluous parts. While creating a framework, it is recommended to stick to the traditional five-paragraph format with an introduction, three body paragraphs, and conclusion.

5. Be creative from the very beginning. The majority of sources devoted to the writing of expository essays emphasize that expository essays are "not meant to be opinionated pieces, so introductions that include a personal plight – as is the usual fare when asked to write an essay — are out of the question" (How to Write an Expository Essay, 2015). Nevertheless, a good start is always the key to success — if the reader will become interested in the work from the very beginning, they will read the rest of the paper as well. So, in consideration of the fact that you cannot use some personal thoughts, the possible way to attract attention is to cite some historical topics or significant issues. No matter what it will be, a significant discovery or study will give you more points from the audience.

6. Write the body of the essay. It was already mentioned that thinking ahead about future arguments is essential while writing an expository essay. At this stage, every idea should be turned into paragraphs, which together form an eloquent but concise body. It is recommended to write two arguments supporting your idea and one counterargument (this part is optional — however, showing the opposite approach will interest a large audience). Do not forget that every argument and counterargument should have an actual basis.

7. Write the conclusion. Some students find conclusion writing to be one of the easiest stages of essay writing, while others have had the time to understand that writing a great conclusion is a challenge. This stage is not simply a retelling of the whole paper, and you cannot just paraphrase your introduction. The best definition of a conclusion for an expository essay may be formulated as the answer to "the questions you have brought out in the reader through the introduction while calling back the arguments you have laid out" (How to Write an Expository Essay, 2015). For an excellent expository essay, show all your analytical skills!

8. Edit and check the essay. This last stage is traditional for any type of essay writing and deserves your attention — I know you want to omit it, but still, please, complete every step if you want to write an excellent paper. Read the prepared expository essay twice. The first time is needed solely to understand whether all parts are in place, if there are some excesses that should be cut off, and if the essay has its logic. Do not forget to check once again all the facts, citations, and statistics— every piece of information you cited. Now, you are ready to read your piece of writing once again and praise yourself for an excellent job!

Guidelines and Tightening Your Essay

This part of the guide is traditionally started with useful tips related to the topic choice for the best paper, as the wrong approach may nullify all of the work done. So, the first piece of advice is to be sure that the chosen topic has enough material to talk about as well as potential interest for the readers (particularly your audience). There are two basic rules while deciding the topic for your expository essay:

- Be in trend! Ask yourself: are there hot issues or some that are discussable? Maybe you notice a new trend and want to share your observations. Note — in this case, comparing is a good strategy for wording an argument, especially a collation of past and present.

- Listen to your heart. Even though it sounds like a line from a well-known song, these words can be applied to essay writing as well. Just remember each time you were obliged to write on a topic that causes no interest, and remember how hard it was to come up with every idea and every sentence. I think you will agree that it is much easier to defend a thesis for a topic you are passionate about.

Good Topic Examples

1. Give some advice to freshmen about the best activities to be involved in.

2. What are the best scandals or memorable events in your college's history?

3. Tell about the history of welfare in the United States.

4. What is the history of affirmative action in education? Be specific about its effects.

5. What are the reasons that encourage teenagers to run away?

6. Explain the connection between social media and interpersonal relationships in the modern world.

7. Explain the phenomenon of homelessness and its causes.

8. Think about the situation where women stay with men who physically abuse them. What are the possible reasons for such behavior?

9. What is a black hole and why is it important?

10. Explain what climate change is and how it affects the lives of people on Earth.

11. What is the principle of creating electronic music?

12. What is a 3D bioprinter and how might it change medicine?

13. What are the causes of depression and its spreading in the United States?

14. What is the IQ score of a genius and what does it mean?

15. What is xenophobia and how can it be overcome?

Useful Tips for Writing an Expository Essay

Taking into consideration the fact that, with a high level of probability, you are a student, the advice will be to think about the best way of explaining the material personally for you. To paraphrase this idea, I can say that it is better to imagine that you are a teacher, and you need to explain the material to students with the goal to introduce them to an absolutely new topic.

Do not forget about creativity. Even though an expository essay is traditionally believed to be fact-based writing, it does not mean that you cannot use imagination. Just remember the best lesson in school — I am almost certain that it was not just a boring presentation of a million facts. Just keep in mind that the text needs to be logical and understandable.

Choose information with the maximum level of concentration in the topic. Do not write everything you are familiar with related to the subject. Try to exclude not just superfluous information, but also overly detailed (or extensive) information and facts with pronounced emotional coloring.

Expository essays usually present a relatively narrow topic and, therefore, are quite limited in length. Keep this idea in mind while starting to write the text, and do not waste your time and space for the introduction.

While talking about the stages of writing an expository essay, it was mentioned that the body may include one paragraph with a counterargument for the thesis statement of the essay. Regarding this, it should be highlighted that a counterargument, in any case, does not mean you doubt your position. It just allows you to show readers that there is another approach or view on the topic and you know it, but yet you believe that your point is better (and you can prove it with the use of evidence). Such paragraph just tells the audience that you have a broad mind and have thought about the topic from several perspectives.

The key rule of writing an expository essay is to explain and present every idea in a way that would be desirable and understandable to yourself.

Mistakes to Avoid While Writing an Expository Essay

- Mistakenly giving a synopsis instead of an analysis. This is of importance not just for a critical essay but for expository writing as well. Do not simply restate what is told in different sources, articles, and by various experts. Think and interpret the information to give a simple explanation to your readers.

- Formulating a weak thesis statement. There is a well-known correlation between the thesis and the hook, and they share a level of importance "on which the rest of your essay hangs" (Bennette, 2014). Try to make it as clear and full as possible.

- Plagiarizing someone's works. Every student knows the potentially serious consequences of plagiarism. However, in pursuit of the best result and the wish to appear academic, students usually try to cheat and include thoughts of people they believe to be experts. Moreover, it is not a secret that papers are often written in the last hours before the deadline, so students do not have enough time to cite everything properly.

- Giving less credible testimony than is required. The essay should contain a thesis, synthesis, and analysis backed up by research from credible academic authorities.

- Using unreliable sources. Credibility is essential while writing an expository essay. Of course, nowadays there is no problem in finding anything about any topic of interest. However, only verified information should be used for academic writing.

Being aware of and avoiding these mistakes will improve your essay writing, so you will be able to achieve a higher quality for your papers — at the same time, if you want to be 100% sure, do not forget to explore the final part of this guide and make your expository essay an example for future generations of students.

Expository Essay Writing Checklist

- **Evaluate your topic:** Do you have enough to say, or too much? Do you need to narrow your topic or expand it? Are there enough credible sources to support your arguments on the topic?

- **Evaluate your audience:** What does your audience already know about your topic? Is there anything they want to know? What tone will be the most appropriate for these readers?

- **Check your thesis:** What side did you choose? What are you going to explain, prove, or refute in your paper? Does each argument prove (or refute in the case of counterargument) the main idea of the paper?

- **Analyze your evidence:** Why did you choose this particular information? Does it support each idea? Can you tell for sure that the information is credible?

- **Do not forget about transitions:** Are all the paragraphs and parts of the paper connected with transitions?

- **Evaluate your conclusion:** Did you reveal the topic? Are there questions that still need to be answered? Did you propose any solutions if there are any? What should the reader do or think after reading your paper?

References

Bennette, C. (2014). Common Mistakes to Avoid When Writing an Academic Essay. In *Pro Writing Aid*. Retrieved from https://prowritingaid.com/art/279/Common-Mistakes-to-Avoid-When-Writing-an-Academic-Essay.aspx

CLRC Writing Center. (2007). Structure of a General Expository Essay. Retrieved from https://www.sbcc.edu/clrc/files/wl/downloads/StructureofaGeneralExpositoryEssay.pdf

Merriam-Webster Dictionary. (n.d.). Expository. Retrieved from https://www.merriam-webster.com/dictionary/expository

Expository Essay. (n.d.). In *Essay Writing Tips*. Retrieved from http://www.essay-writing-tips.com/types-of-essays/expository-essay.html

How to Write an Expository Essay. (2015). In *EssayPro*. Retrieved from https://essaypro.com/blog/expository-essay/

Writing an Expository Essay. (2012). In *Academic Help*. Retrieved from https://academichelp.net/academic-assignments/essay/write-expository-essay.html

Sample 1. How to Be a Happy Camper

Nowadays, camping is considered to be a widespread kind of sport. Commonly, it is a method of recreation carried out in isolation, with natural surroundings. Most camping takes place in huge, well-developed campgrounds where people are engaged in activities and the social experience is a primary goal (Hendee & Campbell, 1969). Nevertheless, most of the people would still prefer to be elsewhere in the wilderness, in the place where one can stay alone in the natural environment, which is why it is important to pay attention to several points while camping to take as much advantage as possible of the trip.

To begin with, camping has been estimated as an opportunity to be isolated from the crowded cities, to experience the wild areas of the natural environment, and to leave the complexities of urban life for some time. These conventional camping conditions may still be implemented to some extent, but conditions in popular public campgrounds have changed. The desired result campers want to achieve is not isolation, but pleasure (Tilton, 2006). So to be a happy camper nowadays implies several points which are necessary to take into account when hitting the road into the woods or mountains.

If one is ready to overcome the highest peak, physical preparation is an essential part of any tour. During such a trip, the campers enjoy many of the typical camping activities, such as hiking, swimming and doing sports, so that it becomes not only a cultural element of the backpacking trip, but also a significant tool for survival in case of an emergency (Tilton, 2006). The number of required skills and knowledge can be huge as the camp experience demands much effort. One can avoid aching muscles by training for several weeks before setting off. Furthermore, it is also necessary to do stretching exercises that are appropriate exactly to each individual. The training should also include easy distance running. By the way, participation in a marathon will not be useless for such a trip.

One more point for a camper to be happy is to have a friendly group of people to accompany you that you will be able to share the best memories with later. To experience wilderness does not mean being alone. Certainly, it can be fascinating at times, but loneliness for a long period becomes significantly depressing. Therefore, companionship is the remedy for isolation. The memories of the moments spent together, whether in pleasure or pain, are the constituents that make the trip inspiring and happy. Complete isolation would be exceedingly boring, but being with or chatting to a person can be calming and lessen stress. Moreover, by being able to dismiss thoughts and impressions, harmony in life can be promoted. Sometimes, a person does not have easy access to assistance. Thus it is important to have somebody to rely on. In case of injuries, it would be great to find oneself with the group who are always prepared to deal with any problem (Hendee & Harris, 1970).

To conclude, the experience the camper gets during the trips and climbing mountains is highly valuable and can not be forgotten. Once one feels comfortable enough to make a move to overnights, it is high time to spend weeks or month enjoying the views of the natural sites. Camping can be the best vacation ever with some thorough preparation and training, along with the right way to be an experience to remember. Campers no longer need to abandon many comforts of the city environment to enjoy nature.

References

Hendee, J. C., & Campbell, F. L. (1969). Social Aspects of Outdoor Recreation—The Developed Campground. *Trends in Parks and Recreation*, 10, 13–16.

Hendee, J. & Harris, R. (1970). Foresters' Perception of Wilderness. *Journal of Forestry*, 68(12).

Tilton, B. (2006). *Tent and Car Campers Handbook* (1st ed.). Seattle, WA: Mountaineers Books.

Sample 2. Eating Healthy on a College Student's Budget

To begin with it has to be said that it is rather difficult to eat healthy while living on a college student's budget. As a matter of fact, the amount of money a student has is limited. And eating healthy is rather costly. For example, buying fresh vegetables and fruits is an expensive process especially in winter. Therefore, a lot of students prefer eating junk food, such as McDonald's or KFC, because it is cheaper than eating healthy food cooked at home or going out and eating at cafes and restaurants. That's why there are some tips that will help students all over the world eat healthy with a minimum amount of money spent on the food.

First of all, it must be highlighted that planning is an effective way to eat healthily and to refrain from simultaneous purchases while shopping. Valerie Willyard suggests that "Meal planning can help you make a list to use as a roadmap at the grocery store and get everything you need for all of your meals (4)." (Healthy Eating for College Students on a Budget, 2012) Meal planning is a nice opportunity not to be lost in the variety of the items listed in the shop.

Moreover, it has to be pointed out that making a grocery list will be the most significant step toward eating healthy food, thus preventing the need to buy unnecessary items. Valerie claims that "Making a grocery list helps you stay on task while grocery shopping and avoid impulse buys"(5). (Healthy Eating for College Students on a Budget, 2012) Therefore, it is much better to make a list of the items a student needs to buy to prevent impulsive purchases.

Secondly, it has to be underlined that the seven tips for eating healthy on a college student budget include "buying and cooking fresh food — it's cheaper!, considering buying frozen vegetables in winter, sharing meals with your roommates, choosing generics over brand names, comparing unit prices, pooling your resources together with your roommates, taking advantage of coupons and sales." (7 Tips for Eating Healthy on a College Student Budget, n.d.) Buying and cooking fresh food is the way to improve the life-and-study balance that will influence the quality of the health. Furthermore, sharing meals with the roommates is probably the most effective step to save the money while eating healthily. A cooking schedule in the room provides an opportunity that can be hardly lost to reach the goal and lead a healthy lifestyle. In fact, if a student prefers eating healthy while living on a college student's budget, he or she should take advantage of coupons and sales. There is a great variety of them on the websites of stores. Moreover, this information is updated weekly, thus it is essential to follow the information provided there. Furthermore, it has to be mentioned that frozen vegetables and fruits are a common alternative to fresh vegetables and fruits because, firstly, it is cheaper, and secondly, it is healthier than buying fresh ones. (7 Tips for Eating Healthy on a College Student Budget, n.d.)

Finally, it has to be said that eating healthy food while living on a college student's budget is a complicated task that may require some tips. Firstly, it must be underlined that planning is an effective way to eat healthily and to refrain from simultaneous purchases while shopping. Secondly, making a grocery list will be the most significant step toward eating healthy food, thus preventing the need for buying unnecessary items. In addition, eating healthy on a college student budget may include buying and cooking fresh food, which is a crucial step of improving the life-and-study balance that will influence the quality of health. Thirdly, sharing meals with the roommates is one the most effective ways to save the money and still eat healthily. As a result, all of these pieces of advice, if followed, will be the best alternative to the junk food so popular among students nowadays.

References

Willyard, Valerie. Healthy Eating for College Students on a Budget. (2012). Retrieved from

https://www.med.umich.edu/pfans/docs/tip-2012/budget-0812.pdf

7 Tips for Eating Healthy on a College Student Budget. (n.d.). Retrieved from

http://www.healwithfood.org/articles/eating-healthy-college-student-budget.php

Chapter 7. Informal Essay Writing Guide

During the years in college, students write dozens of papers, which when added together, can occupy an entire room. Of course, this is a joke, but the amount is really great, and a large part of it falls to essays. These pieces, including articles, reports, or just final papers or reports for the specific course in their nature, are formal writings. Even though young people are more familiar with this type, in daily life every person more frequently faces the informal style of writing. If you do not believe it, just remember how many times a day you read blogs, notes, or how often you practice writing in your diary or life journal. So, this guide is devoted to introducing you with the formal side of informal essays.

What's So Special About an Informal Essay?

I completely understand that the last sentence of the introduction can cause some confusion because of the wordplay "formal side of informal," but this guide will lead you through the process of creating an informal essay.

The first thing that you should remember is that pleasure is the main purpose for this style of writing. Pleasure should accomplish each step of creating the essay, from the moment of topic choice until the presentation for the audience, and pleasure is what your readers should feel. Although at first sight, it seems easy to follow this logic, this task is quite challenging, especially concerning the ability to express thoughts freely.

By this time you may catch yourself being happy about the chance to say whatever you like about everything that concerns you in the most suitable form. It is a pity, but I need to disappoint you slightly. Even though the structure is not so rigid, there is a list of distinctive features for an informal essay:

1. The informal essay is the most personalized kind of academic writing, which in turn allows the use of expressions to define your own thoughts, such as, "I think," "in my humble opinion," and "according to my thoughts."

2. The characteristics of informal writing style allow the covering of controversial topics (Informal Essay, n.d.). This means that while writing an informal essay, you can discuss your religious beliefs or your position on abortion, political issues or right to own a gun.

3. Another peculiar feature of informal essays, which also flows out of a personalized writing style, is a similarity with conversation. Some specialists of writing essays, in this case, draw a parallel with talks between friends about politics after they have been drinking for a little bit (Informal Essay, n.d.).

4. Finally, your personality is the first aspect that should be seen for the reader. Of course, any academic essay will contain a personal position or interpretation, but this element is hidden by facts, arguments, authors, and usage of the third person narrative. Informal writing is primarily for the purpose of expressing your own vision and perception.

As you have already understood, informal essay writing style is the one that is most commonly dealt with by young people. Nevertheless, do not forget that it is often used as a part of formal training, and therefore, the defining final mark is quite a common use of such tasks. It is believed that the informal style helps professors to understand the creativity of students while they have freedom.

The latter parts of this guide will help you understand the principle of writing and create the best informal essay if it is assigned to you. On this stage, it is enough to understand that the closest analog is the journalistic style (shorter text, with attention-catching phrases). At the same time, you should not forget that despite its name, formal language is an essential part in this educational situation.

Regarding this, close attention should be paid to some nuances of the genre. Some things were mentioned above; however, some of them will be specified further:

Tone. There is no additional need to repeat for the umpteenth time all of the rules of formal writing. In this particular case, you can pretty much ignore such requirements, especially while addressing the audience. As you have already known, an informal essay is more like a talk with a friend rather than listening to a lecturer in the class; therefore, a relaxed tone of conversation should be used.

Audience and purpose. Of course, the closeness to the audience among other things dictates the use of words and phrases like "you" and "we're." In this case, emotions are the main purpose of writing — this idea should be remembered. It is a well-known fact that an essayist is always familiar with the audience type, which is even more valuable within this kind of writing (Informal Essay, 2017). Regarding this, it should be noted that informal essays have some sort of individual link to the target group of readers, so there is no need for you to confine the audience — your task is to inspire them or to have them know you better.

Hopefully now you have at least some ideas about your task and requirements when being asked to write an informal essay. In the next chapters of this guide, you will be introduced to the structure of informal pieces of writing, the main stages to follow while writing and checking the essay, and some tips on how to make them the best.

Informal Essay Writing Structure

Without any doubt, I can say that this section of the entire guide will be the shortest one, which I think will not be surprising for you as there is already enough information to understand what an informal essay is. Nevertheless, there are some points that I want to clarify regarding the structure of your future papers in this format. Since middle or high school, everyone is taught to know the traditional "5-paragraph essay" which includes the introduction, body, and conclusion parts. These requirements are the basis for all formal essays. In contradistinction, informal types of papers do not have a specific format and can be determined by the author. In other words, there is no conventional way of organizing the thoughts, judgments, and presentation to the readers, as well as there is no agreement about the length of the informal essay. Moreover, it should be noticed that there are no requirements for informal essays to contain strong theses or even thesis statements as such. That is why informal essays are often compared with the concept of personal essays, which are, in fact, one's discrete considerations that are aimed at enjoyment and creativity (Informal Essay, 2017).

The desire of creating friendly relationships between the writer and future readers together with the main objective (the pleasure from the process of reading) dictates the situation when structure gives way to a more exciting presentation of thoughts. However, it does not mean that you can just scratch some ideas in a few hundred words, as the majority of experts are convinced that "a decent informal essay has an easy-going style but requires an active composition, though that composition may be less stern than in a formal paper" (Informal Essay, 2017).

What are the specifics? Unlike other types of writing of which you can face, the process of studying informal essays has a specific style with a less rigid but still precise plan (Informal Essay, 2015). At the same time, the essential elements, along with tone, are personal ideas, observations, experiences, and last but not least, humor.

Remember! At the same time, it is essential not to forget that the informal style of writing, which is observed within this guide, is still an essay, therefore, you should not forget about the informative side of your paper.

To conclude this section, I want to repeat once again that structure is not the most significant element of any informal essay, as the primary purpose of it is to write an informative piece of writing by expressing your own position or opinion. You can even use the fiction format until your readers are interested and susceptible to the content.

Stages of Writing an Informal Essay

I think you are most likely expecting the traditional scheduled step by step instructions on what to do and in what sequence the writing should be done. Nevertheless, I want to disappoint you because, in the case of writing the details in each step for every guide, they will be almost identical. Instead, I want to concentrate on the most challenging stage while coping with the task of writing an informal essay — the topic choice.

It is an informal essay, which means that you are rarely limited thematically or with precise wording of the title — therefore, "the whole world is lying in front of you." Those who adhere to the opinion that freedom of choice only complicates their "academic life" do not realize that such a situation is just an opportunity to choose a topic which is meaningful and interest personally for them. It can be compared with the chance to say your words and make it as profound as possible. Here are some simple steps that will help you to deal with the step that seems almost impossible — starting your informal essay.

1. Determine the purpose of the future essay. Think about the task you were set: whether you need to convince people to share your opinion, or instead want to describe your experience, some places or ideas, or perhaps you need to explain how to make some tasks. Whatever it will be, you should know the potential topics which, of course, meet these goals.

2. List as many subjects in the focus of your interest as possible. The most important issue at this stage is to understand that regardless of the purpose, your interest can be applied to a countless number of themes. So, my advice is simple — look around and find your inspiration. There is no need for evaluation and judgment, just outline the features.

3. Evaluate each of the topics in the list. Of course, the main criteria is in accordance with the purpose. For example, if you need to convince the reader, make sure that you have a passionate attitude toward the issue. So, while assessing the topic, think on your feelings about it. No less significant is your ability to develop a topic in the appropriate way. Therefore, one of the most important factors determining your choice is the number of arguments and ideas related to the "winner."

Now, you are ready to complete all other stages of classical academic writing, holding in memory the features of informal essays, and do not forget to use the useful tips for creating the best informal essay that will be discussed in the next section of the guide.

Guidelines and Tightening Your Essay

Without a doubt you already have enough information to succeed in writing an informal essay; however, there is a collection of useful tips and pieces of advice that will help you to make your essay the one that deserves the greatest praise.

After talking about the stages of writing, you already know that topic choice is one of the most challenging, and at the same time, the most important stages of writing. Here are some examples.

Good Topic Examples

1. The best journey of my life.

2. My religion.

3. The perfect woman, marriage, and divorce.

4. Reincarnation.

5. The celebrities give us bad examples.

6. What makes my parents special?

7. The longest minute in my life.

8. Studying and working: mission impossible?

9. Arranged marriages: do they still work?

10. Terrorism as the challenge of the modern world.

11. Home education as a trend of the twenty-first century.

12. How you would spend a million dollars.

13. The moment when your life changed forever.

14. Living in a society of ambitious people.

15. Being a mother: happiness or responsibility.

Useful Tips for Writing an Informal Essay

- The first issue that will be noticed by potential readers is the title; therefore, you should pay enough attention to the formulation. After deciding what topic will be illustrated in the essay, there is a need to consider the "perfectly self-explanatory wording" of the title (Rawson, n.d.). In this short sentence, or even word phrase, the meaning of the whole text should be incorporated. It will help the reader to understand the expectations and to attract attention to the essay.

- Try to follow the standard five-paragraph format for the structure. Even though structure is not a critical issue in an informal essay, it will be easier for you to orient and to express the ideas to develop the theme.

- Check if each paragraph contains facts — however, try to find the balance. Your words should not seem overly serious in the final version.

- While computing the text, try to stand on a humorous position or at least a friendly presentation style.

- Even though your essay is written in an informal style, do not forget about transitions used to lead into each of the paragraphs or properly citing all of the outside sources used for information.

- The informal essay, as with other formal counterparts, needs a strong and understandable conclusion. Remember that rich content should not be obtained at the expense of a friendly tone.

- One more piece of advice is to end the whole paper with a sentence that stimulates the readers to think further about the raised issues, or at least to think outside the box.

- Finally, each essay, even an informal essay, needs to be proofread and checked with the possible modifications inserted by your professor (some guides to complete the task).

Mistakes to Avoid While Writing an Informal Essay

Close to the end of this guide, some words about common mistakes need to be mentioned. However, taking into account that this guide is devoted to the informal style of writing, I take the liberty to depart from the usual format of such councils. So, below you will find a fun list of "tips on the reverse," otherwise known as "really bad pieces of advice," which is, if you want to get an excellent score, do just the opposite:

- Use more lyrics! It is a well-known fact that lyrics capture the reader's attention. You are writing an informal essay, which sometimes equates to narrative stories — they are full of lyrics. Do not forget to use as many epithets, metaphors, and comparisons as possible.

- The bigger the introductory part, the better the reaction presented by readers. Do not forget about telling the story of your life — who your parents are, why you decided to write this essay, and what has determined the choice of the topic. The introduction occupying half of the text will definitely intrigue the reader.

- Do not give any concrete ideas about the main issue of the essay. Remember, common words are everything! The main point here is to write more on abstract themes and dilute the text with your musings on the topics that come to your mind in association with the main issue.

- If you are bad at working with useless information, you may use the opposite approach. You may fill the essay with facts, such as names of authors, dates, titles of studies, the results of various researches, and local and global news. The readers will definitely be amazed by your erudition and the ability to work with all kinds of information. And do not forget to write the most laconic conclusion, because you are writing the text for an audience that can think on its own and make logical reasoning without much information.

- Another well-known fact is the dependency between the length of the sentence and the author's intelligence. Remember the masterpieces of world literature, where one sentence is written on half a page — be sure, you can do it as well. Do not forget to use smart and incredibly long words together with large and long-winded sentences. This method will help you to become very clever for the reader's opinion.

Follow these tips, and you will be able to write the most "brilliant" essay in your life.

Informal Essay Writing Checklist

- Does the whole essay reveal the topic, which was carefully chosen for your informal essay writing task?

- Does the essay contain a less formal tone than the traditional academic papers?

- Did you use everyday words, slang and colloquialisms, and "you" and "I?"

- Did you check whether you used the first person to address the reader directly?

- Does the essay stimulate readers to raise questions in their minds with the information you have provided?

- Does the essay fit into the framework of the standard five-paragraphs type of structure?

- Is the subject described in an entertaining manner?

- Did you use examples, quotes, diagrams, anecdotes, narratives, and other types of testimony?

Finally, check the essay on the balance between the formal criteria and informality, grammar and punctuation, and of course, originality.

Some believe that informal essays can be described as "fun mixtures of fact and opinion without having too serious of tone throughout the entire paper" (Rawson, n.d.). Answering these questions will be useful for you to write the first excellent paper with the use of the informal writing style. And it is a well-known fact that the first success determines all of the rest, which is why you should do your best now to be a master in the future.

References

Informal Essay. (2015). In *Essay Info Writing Guides*. Retrieved from

http://essayinfo.com/essays/informal_essay.php

Informal Essay. (n. d.). In *Essay-Writing-Tips*. Retrieved from

http://www.essay-writing-tips.com/types-of-essays/informal-essay.html

Rawson, K. (n. d.). Informal Essay Writing Tips. In *How to Write an Informal Essay*. Retrieved

from http://kellyrawson.net/how-to-write-an-informal-essay.html

Sample 1. My Caffeine Addiction

A little Armageddon happens every morning because there is a need to get out of the warm comfort of bed and be ready to fight with all the world. A large number of people in a crowded city are waiting to ruin your day by stealing your wallet or simply being rude; they will try to catch up and bite you when you do not expect it. Hands do not obey you, legs do not obey you, and instead of a logical order in your head, there is a jumble of thoughts. But everything is going to change after your body will get a little help: the first sip of coffee helps you remember where you are and who you are. The second sip of coffee reminds you of the to-do list for the day that begins. The third sip of coffee and you are ready for a battle.

My obsession with coffee is one form of addiction, allowed by our harsh world, which is increasingly trying to regulate any manifestation of my inner self. In contrast to alcohol, tobacco or drugs, humanity creates an incredibly attractive and glamorous image of coffee consumption. A large number of pages on Instagram advertised how beautiful and cool it is to drink coffee on the balcony, in the cafe, in bed. There are notebooks, tablets, cats, and flowers around cups of coffee on those pictures. The only thing that I want to do after watching this visual folklore—to run to Starbucks as fast as I can and order coffee for $4. What a luxury!

The passion of Westerners for coffee is a phenomenon that emerged after a long time of observation of consumption of this beverage in the Arab world. At one time a monopoly on coffee meant big profits and luxury for a country that has been able to "catch" a colony that is suitable for the cultivation of this product (Schivelbusch, 1992). Coffee always means luxury. Therefore, drinking coffee is not only following body requirements and blindly imitating the beautiful pictures from Instagram, but also to take up the great tradition of coffee consumption. Furthermore, love of coffee unites us with Honore de Balzac, who could drink 50 cups of coffee per day, (O'Hare, 2015) and even with Bach and Beethoven.

Coffee can be a part of a little ritual that we do together with our parents, relatives and loved ones. Let us face it, the awareness that whatever is happening in the world, you will meet your mother for lunch, where you two will slowly drink coffee with a delicious cake, instills a love to the world and banishes the sense of hopelessness and fear of each following day. It is pleasant to talk about secrets and remember the events of the past days over a cup of coffee. Discussions inspire emotions; coffee invigorates body and mind. And last but not least, drinking coffee in a hipster's cafe with your loved one is a luxury.

Unwillingness to recognize the realities of the world and escaping into Instagram and posts on Facebook which begin with the words: "Today, when I drink coffee..." bring a strong desire to be a part of this world that is drinking coffee so public and revealing. I know that coffee does not like me, but I have no idea if I really love coffee. Perhaps it appears in my life under the pressure of our visual world and gives me a chance to feel myself a part of the community that adores coffee. I do not know. But I am addicted to feeling that I am not alone.

References

O'Hare, B. (2015). Honoré de Balzac's Fifty Cups of Coffee. *The New Yorker*. Retrieved from http://www.newyorker.com/humor/daily-shouts/what-i-assume-honore-de-balzac-thought-after-drinking-each-of-his-fifty-daily-cups-of-coffee

Schivelbusch, W. (1992). *Tastes of Paradise* (1st ed.). New York: Pantheon Books.

Sample 2. What Makes Your Mom or Dad Special

Since my earliest childhood, I could find support in my parents and they were always ready to lend me a helping hand. My mom and dad were my friends, my soul mates, who accepted and respected all my interests and initiatives. They have brought me up as a strong individual, confident to express my own opinion and independent of judgment. My father contributed a lot to me being who I am now.

I have always considered my dad special. Even after my graduation from university, he cherishes me like a child, and this care and attention helps me to feel myself young and full of energy. I am confident that I will never be alone in this world, whatever happens. As Sherman Alexie once wrote: "I think all of us are always five years old in the presence and absence of our parents."

My father is a policeman, and since I remember myself, I have been proud of him. Devoting his own life to people's safety and social order is a big deal. When my dad was staying on work till late, I was always worried. Once, he came home late again with a plaster of Paris bandage on his arm. When we wondered what had happened, he told us that it was an ordinary bruise and we had no reasons to worry.

Next morning when we were having breakfast, my mother put a newspaper in front of me. "Policeman saved a child from the fire," the headline said. Only after that my father humbly told about the accident. He was returning home from work when he became a witness of a terrible fire in the house. The fire guards had not arrived yet, and there was a group of people standing in front of the house. The house was all aflame, and he was the only one brave enough to check if anybody was inside. I was very proud of him, but I could not understand why he had not told us about that case the day before. But later, this incident let me understand that it is not always necessary to demonstrate how brave you are. He taught me that if a deed is of valor, there is no sense in praising yourself.

Dan Pearce in his book *Single Dad Laughing* expressed a wonderful idea about fathers being an example how their children should be treated: "Dads. It's time to show our sons how to properly treat a woman. It's time to show our daughters how a girl should expect be treated." I will never stop saying thanks to my father for treating my mother and me with love and solicitude. He managed to raise me as a confident person and now I clearly know what people I want to surround me.

To make a long story short, I want to say that my dad will always be unique for me. I am deeply convinced that I will always feel myself a beloved little daughter and I will show him not by words, but by actions that I will never let him down.

References

Alexie, S. (2008). *The Absolutely True Diary of a Part-Time Indian* (1st ed.). Prince Frederick, MD: Recorded Books.

Pearce, D. (2011). *Single Dad Laughing* (1st ed.). Createspace.

Final Thoughts

Though this section is technically the last, we are not going to say good-bye. While studying, you will need to use this book often. For this reason, there's no need to bid farewell. The only thing we would like to wish you in these final thoughts is to be strong, because only strong people can cope with all the challenges that will be faced while studying.

Our book won't solve all your writing problems if you don't put effort into mastering writing. Therefore, we wish for you to be motivated and inspired. That way, you will be able to complete all your papers quickly and easily. When it's hard to deal with a certain paper, hopefully you'll remember our book and look for ways to solve your troubles in *Essay Becomes Easy. Part II*.

Made in the USA
Monee, IL
04 June 2022

97480160R00062